# GIRLS SPORTS ACADEMY

## Gymnastics

LAURA SIEVEKING

PENGUIN BOOKS

PENGUIN BOOKS

UK | USA | Canada | Ireland | Australia
India | New Zealand | South Africa | China

Penguin
Random House
Australia

Penguin Random House Australia is part of the Penguin Random House group of companies whose addresses can be found at global.penguinrandomhouse.com.

First published by Random House Australia in 2017
This edition published by Penguin Books, an imprint of Penguin Random House Australia Pty Ltd, in 2024



Cover illustrations by Rebecca King © Penguin Random House Australia Pty Ltd
Cover design by Caroline Lee © Penguin Random House Australia Pty Ltd
Internal design and typesetting by Midland Typesetters, Australia

Printed and bound in Australia by Griffin Press, an accredited ISO AS/NZS 14001 Environmental Management Systems printer

NATIONAL LIBRARY OF AUSTRALIA
A catalogue record for this book is available from the National Library of Australia

MIX
Paper | Supporting responsible forestry
FSC www.fsc.org FSC® C018684

ISBN 978 1 76162 030 0 (Paperback)

Penguin Random House Australia uses papers that are natural and recyclable products, made from wood grown in sustainable forests. The logging and manufacture processes are expected to conform to the environmental regulations of the country of origin.

penguin.com.au

We at Penguin Random House Australia acknowledge that Aboriginal and Torres Strait Islander peoples are the Traditional Custodians and the first storytellers of the lands on which we live and work. We honour Aboriginal and Torres Strait Islander peoples' continuous connection to Country, waters, skies and communities. We celebrate Aboriginal and Torres Strait Islander stories, traditions and living cultures; and we pay our respects to Elders past and present.

*For the real Abby, with all my love*

# CHAPTER *One*

Do you remember the day that changed your life forever? I sure do. I still get chills when I think back to it. Don't get me wrong, I've had plenty more days which have freaked me out since then, but this particular day was the one that would make all my future freak-out days possible. Sounds like a bad thing, right?

I remember the silence – it wrapped itself around me like a blanket. My little finger twitched nervously at my side. That was new.

I tried to remain still but it was impossible against the sea of nerves. Suddenly, I heard the music blast through the speakers. I don't know why it made me jump – I was waiting for it. My body leapt to life like a sleeping cat that had its tail stepped on. I'd heard this music a thousand times before but this time was different.

I leapt through the air, light and free – like I could fly. My dance elements matched in perfect unison with the music. I remember stopping in the far left corner of the blue matting. I lowered my arms to my side and took a deep, deep breath. On cue, I sprung forwards, sprinting with all my might. I threw my arms out and launched into my first tumbling row. It was a forward tumbling row. I hate forward tumbling. You'd think tumbling backwards would be scarier, right? Not so. There's a certain amount of momentum to travelling backwards. But forward tumbling always meant I was landing blind. I was never quite sure about where the ground was. And that can be a problem.

I hurled myself into a forward layout. I then went straight into another followed by a somersault which I landed heavily. But I was on my feet and that is what counted. The crowd cheered. I continued with the routine that I could do in my sleep. I could recite it to you in words without taking a breath – split leap, split change leap, tour jeté with a half twist. Handstand, lever down to splits, push through, V-sit up to feet. The words ran through my head to the beat of the music. They fit like lyrics to a song I had written myself. I leapt towards the corner and took a deep breath, ready for my second tumbling run.

The second run was a backward tumble, which made me smile. It was my easiest one and I was confident I'd stick it. I pumped my arms as I launched myself into a round-off. The round-off is what gives you the pace and momentum for the following tricks. I pushed hard through my shoulders and added on a backflip followed by a full twisting layout. I landed gracefully and threw my arms to the side, as wide as my beaming smile.

So far so good. I felt elated and beautiful – this is what I loved about gymnastics. But there was one tumbling row to go and it was the hardest. It was another backward tumbling row (happy days!) but it ended with a double backward somersault. Sound scary? It is. Rotating through the air in a ball two times before landing is no easy task. It required as much height off the mat as possible and a tight, quick turn. I imagined myself soaring through the air and landing it perfectly. The power of visualisation, as Coach Simon would say. I stared down the diagonal of the mat. My vision became a tunnel, focusing solely on the row ahead. The music reached its crescendo and I knew it was time. I could hear muffled voices calling, 'You can do it, Abby!' *You can do it, Abby*, I whispered.

I threw myself forwards into my round-off. I punched out a fast, strong backflip in the build-up to my final double sommie. I pushed hard off the ground and wrapped myself into a tight ball. I groaned slightly from the exertion. As I finished my second rotation, I could tell I was far too low. I barely opened out of my somersault as I felt the ground below me. I landed with my toes, knees and hands on the mat. I spluttered in shock and exhaustion. That was counted as a fall and I was going to lose a lot of points. I picked myself up off the mat and finished the final twirl in my routine. Tears began to sting my eyes. I presented to the judges with a wavering smile as I tried to swallow the lump of sadness in my throat. The crowd cheered enthusiastically and I could see my mum waving from the gallery. I had given it my all. I straightened out my leotard and shook my hands. I lowered my head and tried to cough the tears away.

Simon gave me a firm pat on the back and put his arm over my shoulders. 'Good work, Abby.' He smiled sympathetically. But I knew he was as disappointed as I was.

'There go my chances,' I spluttered.

'Nah,' he said, swiping his hand to the side. 'You've had a great competition, Abs. One fall on floor isn't going to end it all, you know.'

I sniffed. Maybe Simon was right. But this was the biggest comp of my life. Every other competition I'd ever competed in was nothing compared to this one. If I stuffed up any of the others, I'd get over it and prepare for the next one. But there was no 'next one' in this case. This was it. Make it or break it. I slipped on my tracksuit and gulped down some water from my bottle. The results and presentation would begin shortly, including the big announcement.

My mum rushed over from the other side of the gallery until she was standing directly above me. 'I'm so proud of you!' she squealed.

I smiled nervously and I could tell she was feeling my disappointment.

Slowly, the gymnasts gathered on the centre of the floor as the judges arranged the podium. First. Second. Third. This was the first time I couldn't care less about the podium. All I wanted to hear was the big announcement. I sat nervously bouncing my knee as the presentations were made for each division. I even placed third on bars and second on beam. But that didn't guarantee me anything. As I jiggled my knee my new medals clinked and chimed around my neck like a soundtrack to my tension.

'And now, the announcement you've been waiting for,' the head judge said as she smiled into the microphone. 'The following girls have placed high enough to be accepted into the Academy of Sport for Girls,' she proclaimed. It felt like the list rolled on forever. Name after name, followed by squealing and hugs all around me. 'Claudia Cox, Mae Choon, Abigail Rogers, Sophie ...'

My heart skipped a beat. Was that right? Could she read it again? Did she say Abigail Rogers? The room began to spin as I whirled around, looking for some kind of confirmation of what I'd heard. I gazed up to the gallery and there was my mum, jumping up and down and wiping tears from her eyes. *You did it!* she was mouthing.

I shook my head. I couldn't believe it. I knew it was one of those moments. One that would change my life from here on in. I had been accepted into the Academy of Sport for Girls – the most prestigious sports school in the country. I'd been training for this for years and I was finally in. I was in! A school where you did your schoolwork but also where you trained long and hard. National champions came out of this school, not to mention the best coaches in the country.

*Academy of Sport – here I come!*

# CHAPTER *Two*

The summer passed in a blur. I remember my friends chattering about starting high school together. I felt left out. They were all going to the same school and here I was trekking across the city to get to my new school. But not even that could dampen my excitement. In just six weeks, I would be at the Academy of Sport for Girls.

The first day of school came around in a whirl. One minute I was hugging my friends goodbye at my farewell party and the next I was standing nervously in front of the school gates. I felt my mum squeeze my shoulder lightly as we stood gazing into my future. The large sign towered above me at the entrance. *The Academy of Sport for Girls – Creating champions for over fifty years.* Butterflies danced around my stomach. *Creating champions*, I mouthed. Would that be me? Was I the next champion?

Mum gently tugged the sleeve of my school blazer, nudging me through the gates. We walked through the grounds of the school. There were girls everywhere. It was a big school – much bigger than my little primary school. My eyes widened in wonder at the towering buildings among huge open fields. Some girls carried netball bags, others hockey sticks. I even saw girls wearing jodhpurs walking down to the equestrian stables. This school had it all. We followed the arrows which directed new students to various areas of the campus. We passed a sign pointing towards the 'Boarding Quarters'. Not only was this school a huge sports academy, but it was also a boarding school for girls who lived far away from the city. I'd heard a lot of the boarders came from the country for the equestrian program. I was quietly glad I wasn't a boarder – it was hard enough starting a new school all by yourself, let alone having to *live* there.

New students had been asked to go to the Assembly Hall first. Even though we were all starting Year 7, some of the girls seemed to tower above me. Basketballers, I thought.

Everyone seemed to know somebody. But I didn't. I noticed nobody had their mums with them and I suddenly felt really daggy. 'Mum, you can go now,' I whispered.

Mum turned to me with a look of surprise. 'Really? Are you sure?'

I nodded. 'I'll be fine!' But inside I just wanted my mum to wrap her arms around me like a baby. Mum gave me a quick squeeze and headed back towards the school gates. I hovered by the wall, watching as all the other girls chattered happily. I nervously looked down at my blue and white striped summer dress. I gently smoothed my hands over my thighs, even though I knew Mum had already ironed out any wrinkles. I felt hot in the very formal school blazer, which was like a coat you would see on a businesswoman in the city. At my old school, we never had a blazer.

I turned to my left and saw another girl standing by herself. I could immediately tell she was a gymnast. Gymnasts have such obvious nervous traits. She was standing on one foot, casually stretching out her ankle on the floor. Textbook. She also jiggled her arms as if trying to keep them warm in a competition. She shook out her hands and bounced lightly on her toes as if preparing for a vault run. Clearly petrified. I realised

I recognised the girl. She had been in the competition round with me before summer. She had long, straight black hair pulled neatly back in a plait, dark skin and a tiny little frame. She looked over at me and smiled. I picked up my bag and wandered over.

'Hi,' I chirped. 'I'm Abby.'

'Abby Rogers, yeah, I know.' She grinned. 'Good job on the audition comp. You nailed your beam routine. Amazing!'

'Oh, thanks,' I stammered. 'What's your name?'

'I'm Mae. Mae Choon. Do you know anybody here?'

'Nup. You?'

'Nup. I guess we're in the same boat.' She smiled.

'Attention, everyone,' a voice boomed from the stage. 'Could you all please come and take a seat so we can begin?'

Mae picked up her bags and casually linked her arm into mine and pulled me towards the chairs. I smiled lightly. As I sat down, I scanned the room around me. It was vast. There were rows and rows of tiered seats facing a stage. There must have been two or three hundred girls sitting in the room – more than my entire primary school! This was only Year 7 as well. Some of the girls were tall and broad. Others were petite and tiny. But everyone seemed to have one thing in common – a nervous smile and a look of hope and ambition in their eyes.

As I looked up at the stage, I could see the Academy crest shining brightly on the podium which an important-looking lady was standing behind. It was the same logo printed on our sports t-shirts, our blazer pocket, our school-bags and many other items from the Academy. The crest was in the shape of a shield, divided into four quadrants. In each quadrant was a different icon, representing a quality of an Academy girl. There was a lion, symbolising strength. The second quadrant showed an eagle, which symbolised spirit and nobility. The third quadrant had a plume of feathers, which signified service to others. And the last was the laurel leaves which meant triumph. Underneath the shield was a ribbon which had the Latin words *Luceat lux vestra*, which means *Let your light shine.* I felt my heart swell in my chest as I read over the words.

'Welcome to the Academy of Sport for Girls! I am Mrs Brunette, the principal of the college.' I breathed in deeply through my nose as those words echoed in my ears. It felt like a dream.

'Good mor-ning, Mrs Bru-neeeeettte,' the girls chorused.

'Now, each of you is here because you earned your place. You have proven to us that you are among the top sportswomen in the country. But this is just the beginning. Now you are here, you need to keep earning your place day by day. Listen to your coaches. Train hard. But do not neglect your studies. You are elite sportswomen and that comes with a unique pressure. Most girls your age only have to worry about getting their homework done on time. But you have to balance your academics and your sport. You will have competitions clashing with assignments. You will face nerves in the gym or on the field, the track or the pool, as well as in the classroom. But managing these aspects of your lives is where the true test will be.' Everyone sat silently staring at Mrs Brunette. Each girl in the room had the one same dream. To make it as a world-class sportswoman. But we also all knew that that would only be a reality for a select few.

Next, a tall girl, obviously a senior, stood up to the podium. 'My name is Elise Goldburn and I am your school captain,' she said brightly. 'And, yes, I'm a swimmer,' she said cheekily. A few girls in the row behind us let out a cheer. I turned around and saw the broad-shouldered girls laughing confidently. Clearly swimmers.

‘Now it’s time for you to go off to your various sports and meet your head coaches,’ Elise said. She then listed each sport and directed the students to where they would be meeting. Gymnasts were to gather in the foyer of the gymnasium.

Mae and I gathered our gear and followed the signs down to the gymnasium. It seemed like the smallest girls had broken off from the main assembly and were headed down to the gymnasium. The swimmers ran off with a cheer and the equestrian girls walked away with a sense of grace and dignity.

We arrived in the gymnasium foyer and sat down on the floor. Suddenly, a woman with dark hair and dark eyes made her way to the front of the room. A few girls gasped. It was head coach, Ana Petrescue. There wasn’t a girl in the room who hadn’t heard of Ana. She was renowned for her rigorous training programs. She was a hard coach but she was the best. She had produced many of the finest gymnasts in the country, some of whom had gone on to win Olympic medals.

'Good morning!' Ana said energetically. 'Welcome to your first day at the Academy,' she continued. 'This is the first day of the rest of your sporting career. My coaches and I are tough; I'm sure you've heard that,' she said with one eyebrow raised. A few of the girls giggled. 'But we are here to make each of you the best gymnast you can be. We are here to make you grow. We are here to make you fly.'

Something inside my chest swelled. I felt happy and nervous all at the same time.

'Okay, go and find your lockers and get changed. Training session one begins now.' Everyone looked around slightly confused. We hadn't expected to be thrown into a training session in the first hour of arriving at the Academy. Nobody moved.

'I said NOW!' Ana bellowed. 'Be back here in the gym in ten minutes. Anyone late will be running laps all afternoon. The change rooms are downstairs. GO!' At that the girls sprung to life. Each girl jumped up and took her bags, running for the locker rooms. Mae grabbed my arm and we raced down the stairs, following the stampede of gymnasts. I suddenly felt a little panicky.

The change rooms were buzzing like a beehive. Mae and I found an empty spot on one of the benches and dumped our bags down heavily. All around us girls whipped off their uniforms and suddenly the room became a rainbow of colourful leotards. Pink swirls, metallic blues, satin ribbons and soft crushed velvet purples paraded out of the change room as the girls ran for the gym. I reached frantically around my bag, searching for my leotard. Mae pulled her bright green leo over her crop top and looked nervously at me. 'C'mon, Abby, we've gotta run,' she said, frowning.

I threw my tracksuit top from my bag. I pulled out my lunch, my water bottle and some notebooks for school. Where was my leotard? I found bike pants, but that wasn't going to be helpful if I had no top.

'Please wait for me, Mae!' I pleaded.

Mae jittered her legs. 'Abby, I r-r-really don't want to be late,' she stammered. I turned my bag upside-down and the final contents spilled onto the bench. But there was no leotard.

'Mae, what am I going to do?' Mae shook her head lightly and tried to smile sympathetically. My eyes began to fill with tears. My stomach felt like I'd done 100 giants around the high bar in a row.

'Hey,' a voice said from behind us. Mae and I turned to see a girl calmly folding her dress on the bench. She was taller than both of us and had an air of knowingness about her. She had on a plain black leotard with ornate crisscrossing straps on the back. She reached into her bag and pulled out a purple lump of material. She rolled it into a ball and threw it to me. I caught the ball and opened it up. It was a purple crop top that I could wear with my bike pants.

'Oh my goodness, thank you so much,' I mumbled as I quickly yanked the crop top on. But the girl was already walking out of the change rooms.

'Don't sweat it,' she called over her shoulder.

Mae and I bolted for the gym and scurried inside just as Coach Ana was lining everyone up in a row. She raised one eyebrow and said 'Just made it,' as we bundled into line. Ana went along the line with her clipboard, checking off each person's name. As she ticked off their name, she told each person to go and sit in one of four different groups. Suddenly, there was a bang and everyone startled. Ana frowned and turned to the door. It was the girl in the black leotard. How had she managed to come in after us?

'You are late,' Ana said coldly.

'Sorry, coach, I just had to fill my water bottle,' the girl in black replied.

'That's no excuse. What is your name?'

'Scarlet.'

'Scarlet who?'

Scarlet paused.

'Surname. NOW, or you can get out of my gym,' Ana bellowed.

Scarlet thought for a minute. She cleared her throat and said loudly and precisely, 'Scarlet Belyakov.' Ana raised an eyebrow.

'Well, Miss Belyakov. I hope you don't think there are different rules for you, just because of who you are.'

Scarlet stared at Coach Ana. She silently took her place in the line with her head raised high and a stony expression on her face.

'Is that ...' Mae began to whisper to me as I nodded. It had to be her. Nobody else had a name like that.

# CHAPTER *Three*

Mae and I squealed with delight when we found out we were in the same training group. We were in a group of eight girls and rotated around the different coaching staff. It just so happened that our first session was with Coach Ana herself.

I took a second to check out my surroundings. This gym was much bigger and better than my old one. There were rows of beams against the right-hand wall – high beams, middle-sized beams and a beam which was only inches off the floor. In front of the beams there was the bars circuit. Several sets of uneven bars stood row by row with blue matting around them. Buckets of chalk sat waiting beside each set of bars. In the centre of the gym was the world-class floor. It was a sprung floor, as all world-class floors are. They're not like trampolines or anything – when you stand on it, it feels slightly spongy under your feet. But the only way to get the amazing spring out of it is to hit it with great force. If you tumble hard, you fly high! There were several other rows of mats for tumbling, including a long, slim trampoline built into the floor. I couldn't *wait* to have some fun on that. Behind the floor area was a large foam pit. It was filled with hundreds of foam cubes and it was used to practise new tumbles and dismounts from the bars suspended above it. It was so fun to be able to do huge dismounts and tumbles and know that you were landing in something as soft as a cloud. To the far right were the vaulting tables with several springboards leading up to them. There were also various stretch and strength areas and even a ballet barre along the wall with full-length mirrors beside them.

I breathed in sharply. Even though this was a totally new gym, it still had the same smell as all the gymnastics gyms I'd ever been in. It's a strange kind of smell – a mix of chalk, sweat and the rubber underside of the matting. But to me, it smelled like home.

Mae and I warmed up with the other girls in our group, giving nervous smiles. Two of the girls came and sat in the splits beside us.

'I'm Evie,' beamed the girl next to me. She was a tall, strong-looking gymnast. She had long blonde hair pulled neatly into a bun and her blue eyes sparkled. Her leotard was a bright display of neon rainbow colours. Her cheeky smile was absolutely contagious.

'And I'm Anwen,' the other girl said quietly. She had dark brown – almost black – hair which contrasted with her smooth pale skin. She was a tiny little thing with light blue eyes and an elfin nose. Her leotard was a sea of blues and greens, rolling together in swirling patterns.

'Did you see Scarlet Belyakov is in our year?' gasped Evie, pointing to the other training group. We glanced over and saw Scarlet warming up separately from her group. She looked fierce and determined. 'I wonder if her sister will ever come and visit the gym!'

'I would love to meet her one day,' Anwen said shyly. 'Scarlet's sister, Katherine, was my absolute favourite gymnast. I remember watching her in the last Olympics – her floor routine was amazing.' We all nodded in awe as we remembered what was dubbed one of the most flawless floor routines ever witnessed in an Olympic Games.

'Scarlet looks so ... angry,' Mae said as she scrunched up her nose. 'I wonder if she even *likes* being a gymnast.'

'Maybe she feels forced into it because of her sister,' Evie said thoughtfully.

'Maybe it's because she's not that good,' another voice said from behind us. We spun around to see a girl standing with her hands on her hips. She had an air of confidence about her as she spoke with one eyebrow raised. She was wearing a pink crushed velvet leotard with a silver metallic swirl which wrapped itself around her small but muscle-toned body. Her dark hair was pulled back tightly in a high ponytail with a plait running down her back. She had olive skin and amazing cat-green eyes.

'What's your name?' I asked as I stretched my legs.

'Bella Burnetti,' she replied shortly. 'I thought you might have known that already.' I frowned at the others, puzzled.

'Why would we …' Mae began when Bella interrupted her.

'Bella Burnetti. National Junior Champion. Did you not make it to Nationals last year?' she asked coolly.

'Oh. No, I missed out, but congratulations on your title,' Mae said sheepishly.

Bella turned abruptly and walked towards a stack of foam blocks. They were piled one on top of the other and reached Bella's belly button as she stood next to them. Glancing around the room, she put one foot on top of the stack of blocks and slowly sunk down into the splits. It was the biggest over-split I'd ever seen. Bella looked around casually as if it were the easiest thing in the world.

'Bella, over here, please,' a voice said firmly from behind us. 'I said to warm up as a group, not wander off around the gym.'

Bella jumped up. 'Sorry, Coach Ana. I just wasn't finding anything to help me stretch. I'm just *too* flexible sometimes!'

'Well, I hope you have the strength to back

that up, Bella. Super flexible gymnasts can often be too floppy.'

Evie jabbed me in the side, hiding a smile. I burst out laughing. Bella turned sharply towards me and narrowed her eyes. I immediately stopped smiling. Bella prowled over and leaned closely into me. 'I saw your audition comp,' she whispered. 'Nice stack on floor. I'm surprised you even got into the Academy.' Bella walked off in a huff, leaving me feeling like I had swallowed a stone.

'Okay, everyone, up. Girls, we're going to start with some tumbling today. Make a line at the end of the tumbling mat and we'll go through the basics right up to the hard stuff,' Coach Ana said, pointing to the tumbling mats. One by one, we performed each of the tumbling rows requested. It started easy – basic round-offs, backflips, handsprings and sommies. But with each row, Coach Ana added a new level of difficulty. The pace was fast – there certainly wasn't any chatting between tumbling rows. I began to puff hard but didn't want anyone to know I was tiring so quickly on the first day.

'Bella,' Coach Ana yelled from the end of the mats, 'Round-off, two backflips, layout.'

'Okay!' Bella took off and punched out a forceful round-off. Her two flips were fast and furious. Then she soared through the air into her layout. A layout is like a somersault in the air but your body is straight. For that moment, Bella looked like she was suspended in the air. I could see a light flicker of a smile on her face as she gracefully landed on the mats. Coach Ana gave a brief nod of approval. Bella beamed.

'Anwen, go!' shouted Coach Ana. Anwen raced, her tiny arms and legs pumping. She launched into her round-off with a huge amount of power for such a little thing. 'Wow, pocket rocket!' Coach Ana smiled at the end of Anwen's tumbling row. Anwen's cheeks reddened in embarrassment. Evie high-fived her as she returned to the line.

'Abby, go!' Coach Ana yelled. I pumped my arms and launched into my round-off. As I started to punch out my first flip, I heard Bella mumble as she walked back to the line, 'Eew, messy!' In that split second my mind filled with doubts. What was messy? What was I doing wrong? What was Coach Ana thinking? My flips started to veer off course. My layout was low and sloppy and I landed heavily and unbalanced. I staggered to the side and toppled over, bumping straight into Coach Ana. She fell with a thud onto her bottom. The gym went silent.

'I'm so sorry,' I mumbled as I jumped to my feet, 'I don't know what happened – I just lost . . .'

'You lost focus,' Coach Ana finished for me as she dusted herself off. I couldn't read her expression – was she angry? 'There's no room for lack of focus in my gym,' she said sternly. My heart sank. 'But I also have excellent hearing,' she said, raising an eyebrow. 'Bella?'

Bella looked up. 'Ten laps, round the gym. Now. We are a team and there's no room for sabotage in my team!' Bella's eyes were wide and she opened her mouth to argue but clearly thought better of it. Mae smiled cheekily behind her.

I couldn't believe I'd just knocked over one of the best gymnastics coaches in the country. I felt like I wasn't good enough to be there. Bella was right – it was obvious I was rubbish compared to the others. I was so used to being the best in my club and here I was with some of the top junior gymnasts in the country.

After our floor work we rotated to beam. I was usually pretty good at beam, but I just wasn't myself. I wobbled on the easiest moves and found myself falling off and jumping back onto the beam time after time. The other girls waited patiently through our drills while I re-mounted the beam for about the fiftieth time. Bella rolled her eyes constantly and Coach Ana frowned, as though thinking hard about something. She was probably wondering how on earth I got accepted into the Academy.

'Okay, drinks break. Go get your water bottles and take five,' Coach Ana shouted. 'Abby,' she called out and turned to face me, 'come see me for a minute.'

Mae gave me a reassuring smile but I felt like I had a pile of pebbles sitting in the bottom of my stomach. I walked over, taking a deep breath. Was this the end of everything for me? Was I going to be kicked out of the Academy on the first day?

Coach Ana narrowed her eyes as she looked at me. I stared down at my feet, unable to meet her gaze.

'Abby, you know I was at the Academy trial before summer,' she said slowly. I nodded. 'I've seen you compete. You are a good gymnast – a strong gymnast. You know, you were one of the few girls that stood out to me.

I remembered your name and was excited that you made it into the Academy.'

I looked up, surprised. 'You remembered me? Why?'

'Your floor routine was beautiful. You aren't just a gymnast who does the moves and keeps it neat. You are expressive. I can see how you love gymnastics. You feel the music and when you fly through the air, you truly soar. You look so … so free. But today? Where has that gymnast gone? You're clunky and unbalanced and you look like you don't even want to be here.'

'Oh, I do, Coach Ana, I really do. I just wonder if I'm actually good enough to be here.' Tears began to fill my eyes.

'What is it you love about gym?' Coach Ana asked.

I thought for a moment. 'I think it's what you said before. About being free. When I'm swinging through the air on the bars or leaping high off the beam or soaring through my tumbling rows, I feel like a bird. I feel like there's nothing else in this world – like nobody can touch me.' I hung my head, worried that I sounded stupid.

'That's it, Abby,' Coach Ana said softly. 'That's the passion. You need to forget about what everyone else is doing and hold onto that passion. Be confident. You are here for a reason. Sure, there may be other gymnasts who have Olympians in the family or who are National Junior Champions. But that doesn't mean they have the heart. You have the heart. So stop doubting yourself.' Coach Ana looked me straight in the eye and patted me on the shoulder. 'Go get a drink.'

As I walked back to the benches a surge of confidence filled me to the core. I straightened my back and walked a little taller. My new friends Mae, Evie and Anwen were huddled together, staring nervously at me.

'It's okay, everyone, I haven't been kicked out of the Academy,' I laughed. I saw the relief wash over my friends' faces. 'Coach Ana just wants me to focus. It's all good.'

'Thank goodness!' Anwen said in her chirpy voice. She linked arms with me and smiled her sweet smile. She was like a little fairy.

'Yeah, thank goodness. We need more *normal* people around here,' Evie laughed, her eyes darting in Bella's direction. We all laughed until Bella looked over and we quickly smothered our giggles.

I smiled. With friends like these, I had a feeling I was going to be just fine.

# CHAPTER Four

'See you later, birthday girl!' Mum called as I climbed out of the car.

'Ssssh!' I hissed, looking around, embarrassed. I gave her a quick wave and slammed the car door as I trotted through the school gates.

I walked down the hallway to my locker. A few of the other girls I passed smiled at me cheekily. Odd. As I rounded the corner I could see a bundle of colourful balloons bumping about in the breeze. They were attached to the row of lockers. As I got nearer, I saw they were attached to *my* locker. Oh man, I hope this wasn't something my mother had done. How embarrassing – I'd never live it down. I hurriedly opened my locker so I could start hiding the balloons away. But I got the fright of my life when I saw a cake sitting in my locker with a lit candle! It was lucky my whole locker hadn't caught on fire – what the heck was Mum thinking?

'SURPRISE!'

I jumped out of my skin and spun around to see Mae, Anwen and Evie glowing at me. Evie led a rousing chorus of 'Happy Birthday', much to my delight and embarrassment. When the singing and boisterous cheers finally died down, I shook my head in disbelief.

'Did my mum tell you? How on *earth* did you know it was my birthday?'

'I have a confession,' Mae said cheekily. 'I saw it on your information form which we filled out yesterday. I wasn't being a stalker – I was just checking which gym club you came from and I noticed that it had the next day's date as your birthday. I didn't want you to feel forgotten on your birthday – I hope you don't mind.'

I gave Mae a hug and laughed. 'Of course I don't mind – this is amazing.'

'Anwen made the cake,' Evie said as Anwen's face reddened in embarrassment.

'It's chocolate,' she said, 'I hope you like chocolate.'

'Uh, YES! Cake for breakfast, anyone?' I pulled the cake out of my locker and began slicing a few little pieces with the butter knife next to the cake. The four of us sat down in front of the lockers and greedily began to dive in to Anwen's rich chocolate cake.

'What do you reckon Coach Ana would think about us eating cake right before training?' Evie laughed between mouthfuls. We all shook our heads, dreading to think.

'We shouldn't be stuck inside training on such a gorgeous day anyway,' said Evie. 'We should be at the beach!'

I peered out over the wall which closed in the hallway we were sitting in. It was a glorious summer day with a clear blue sky and the smell of freshly cut grass hung in the air. We were on the second storey so we could see out over most of the Academy. Directly below us were the tennis courts. Tennis players were running drills, belting the ball to and fro over the net. There were six courts lined up in a row, filled with players. To the right was the Assembly Hall where we had met on the first day. It was a towering building which was rounded in shape and had a steep set of stairs leading to its entrance. The wide, glass doors opened out to a huge auditorium of tiered seats which faced a big, deep stage. I remembered looking at the heavy, blue velvet curtains on either side of the stage yesterday and thinking how grand everything here was.

Assemblies took place in there as well as other meetings and concerts. Down the hill led to the ovals. There were three ovals, all with crisp green grass. One had synthetic grass for the hockey players while the other two were manicured grass lawns for the soccer and cricket players.

The grounds of the Academy were huge. From where I was sitting I couldn't even see the gym, aquatic centre or athletics track. Then right down at the bottom of the school were the stables and paddocks for the equestrian students. I hadn't been down there yet, but apparently it housed the beautiful horses that belonged to the girls. Zigzagging throughout the sports fields and arenas were small brick buildings which contained the classrooms. Sometimes you could forget this was a normal school as well as a sporting institution. My bag was already chock-full of textbooks and exercise books for my schoolwork.

Today was what we called a quarter training day. That meant we only had gym training in the morning and the rest of the day was filled with classes. On other days we'd have half training days and one full training day a week on Fridays. Even when we weren't doing sport all day, sometimes we'd also have before or after school training, depending on your sport. My mind was spinning just thinking about the amount of training and school we had to fit into each day . . .

'Sorry, can I get to my locker?' a voice said from above, snapping me back into reality. We glanced up and saw Scarlet Belyakov standing there with her bag.

'Sorry, sure,' we said in chorus, shifting away from the lockers.

'Scarlet, would you like some of my birthday cake?' I asked nervously. There was something about Scarlet that made us all a bit wary. 'For saving my butt in the change rooms yesterday,' I said, half-smiling.

Scarlet hesitated. She began to shake her head but then paused, as if thinking to herself. 'Yeah, okay, why not?' she said and plonked down next to us. I began to cut her a slice. She tucked a strand of her long dark hair behind her ear. She was a solid girl – a very tall and muscly gymnast, like Evie. Anwen looked like a little pixie sitting down next to her.

'So, Scarlet, is your sister, Katherine, fully retired now?' Mae asked.

Scarlet frowned. 'Yeah, pretty much. She coaches now.' Scarlet bit her lip and lowered her dark brown eyes.

'Her floor routine is my favourite Olympic routine I've ever seen,' Anwen said, smiling.

Scarlet took a deep breath and looked up suddenly. 'You know, on second thoughts I think I'll pass on the cake,' she said, standing up. 'Probably not the best thing to eat right before a training session.' Scarlet shoved her bag in her locker and shut it loudly. She walked off swiftly, carrying her water bottle in her hand. 'Later!' she called, without looking back to us.

'What's her problem?' Evie asked. 'She's so rude sometimes.'

I watched her as she walked away – determined and brisk in her strides. 'I dunno,' I said, chewing my last bits of cake. The bell pierced through the air taking us by surprise. Wiping the last crumbs from our mouths, we all jumped up and got our sports bags out of our lockers.

'Let's go,' Evie said and slung her bag over her shoulder. 'If there's one thing I learned yesterday it's that Coach Ana does NOT like lateness!'

We all nodded and hastily gathered our gear and made our way down to the gym.

# CHAPTER Five

Regret. That dark, desperate feeling, wishing you could change a decision you made in the past. I can tell you Evie, Anwen, Mae and I had big regrets about eating that cake right before a training session. And to make matters worse, we were focusing on bars that morning. With each soaring cast came the crash of our bellies back onto the bar. It felt like being punched in the stomach. I groaned with each movement. Thankfully we didn't have Coach Ana that morning. We were working with another coach called Rebecca who, although tough, was not quite as critical as Coach Ana.

I finished my routine with a simple fly-away – a single somersault off the high bar to land on my feet. It was a skill I could do when I was eight.

'Soft option!' frowned Coach Rebecca. But she waved me over to the bench to get a drink as Bella walked up for her turn on the main set of bars. Of course Bella nailed a flawless routine, ending with a 'Woohoo!' from Coach Rebecca. Bella looked around the room to see who was watching, smiling like a Cheshire Cat.

'Glad I didn't pig out on cake this morning,' she sneered as she passed the rest of us at the drinks bench. Evie poked her tongue out.

'I had someone just like her at my old club – a real show-off,' Evie said, shaking her head.

'Which club are you from?' I asked. 'Are you and Anwen boarders at the Academy?'

'Nah, not boarders. We are from Flippers. It's just on the other side of the bridge. Anwen and I have been training there together since we were five. We were both put in the same development squad when we were this high,' she said, holding her hand down by her knee. 'They put Anwen in the squad because she was so flexible and strong.'

'And they put Evie in the squad because she climbed to the top rafter of the gym and wouldn't get down because she didn't want the class to end!' giggled Anwen. 'I reckon they figured any five-year-old that could climb to the roof was destined to become a famous gymnast.'

Evie laughed, pushing Anwen playfully to the side.

Suddenly, a shrill whistle pierced the air. 'Attention, everyone!' yelled Coach Ana. 'Grab a drink and come sit over here on the floor mats – I have something I want to tell you.' We all grabbed our drink bottles and scurried over to the bright blue mats.

'I've been chatting with the other coaches, and while we've seen you in competition and a little in training, we want to work out the best ways to get to know you more as gymnasts. It will mean that we can put you in groups according to your abilities. And the best way to test who will be at the top is simple. A competition.'

The noise rose instantly. A comp? In the first few weeks of the school year? We were all shocked. Some of us had been out of training over summer, and a lot of the girls hadn't competed in over four months. No one was expecting to be in a comp so early. I shook my head, wide-eyed. Mae looked just as shocked as I was.

'Now, don't get worked up,' Coach Ana reassured us. 'It's just an in-house comp. We won't be inviting anyone to compete with you.

But there is some extra motivation for you. The top-twelve gymnasts from this comp will be put into what we will call Squad A. From Squad A we will select the team of six to go on to the first major competition of the year – the State Prelims.'

The State Prelims weren't for months, but we all knew it was the first big meet of the year. I glanced at Evie who nodded confidently at me. How cool would it be if Mae, Evie, Anwen and I made it into Squad A? I could tell the other girls were thinking exactly the same thing.

'And if you're going to compete, there's only one thing you should be wearing.' Coach Ana smiled. Someone behind me squealed with delight. Coach Ana reached into a bag and pulled out the brand new Academy competition leotard. She held it up and everyone around started cheering.

The body of the leotard was a navy blue. Over the top were beautiful white and light blue swirls which snaked their way around the body of the leotard. Tiny little silver beads were sewn on, making the leotard sparkle under the gym lights. Across the very top part of the leotard the material changed to shining white. The white extended down the arms all the way to the wrists. We *oohed* and *aahed* as she passed it around. I was so excited – I couldn't believe I would be wearing an official RASG comp leotard. I was desperate to try one on. Coach Ana began reading out names and tossing the new leos to their owners. I caught the plastic bag she threw to me and I couldn't wipe the smile off my face. I gently released the sticky tape which closed the bag and reached in. I could feel the soft, smooth material against my fingers. I pulled the material out of the bag and unfolded it. The metallic blue and white swirls shone even brighter close-up. I held it up into the light and imagined myself in the leotard, standing on a podium. It was all my dreams coming true. I glanced at Mae who grinned uncontrollably.

'Well, I think this calls for a celebration,' laughed Evie. Mae, Anwen and I swivelled around to face her. 'It's super hot and I think we'll need some cooling off this arvo. Who's up for a swim at my place?'

'Sounds awesome,' I said, gently wiping the sweat from my forehead. It felt like it was about 100 degrees in the gym. 'I'll call my mum later, but I reckon it'll be fine.'

'I'm in,' Anwen smiled.

'Me too,' said Mae.

The bell pierced through the speakers, reminding us that we weren't just gymnasts but school students too.

'Argh, Maths,' whined Evie.

We let out a collective groan and grabbed our gear, heading for the change rooms. It was going to be a long day.

That afternoon we caught the train to Evie's house. She lived on the northern side of the city, which meant a quick train ride over the harbour. She and Anwen both lived quite close to the school which was lucky for them. Mae and I had to travel about forty minutes to get there. Once we got off the train we were able to walk to her place. The afternoon sun was blazing down, soaking into our school dresses. I was carrying my backpack, loaded with textbooks, plus my training bag with all my gear. It weighed a tonne.

'Are we there yet?' I moaned.

'Yep, just across here,' Evie said.

I hadn't really been looking around me – I was concentrating too hard on how heavy my bag was. But when I looked around, I saw a beautiful tree-lined street, surrounded by massive houses.

'This is me!' Evie said, typing in a code to the electronic gates. The gate opened to reveal a massive pebbled driveway which pulled up and around a huge brick house. I glanced over to Mae whose jaw was open in awe. Anwen of course was completely unfazed – she'd been friends with Evie for years and had probably been there a thousand times.

'Your house is enormous,' I said, wide-eyed.

Evie shrugged and opened the front door with her key. We entered into a formal lounge room with a big grand piano in the corner.

'Okay, follow me, we'll get changed in the pool house.' Evie led us through the huge kitchen to the back of the house where the luxurious pool house was.

I wandered over to the bay window and glanced outside. It overlooked the garden – a massive area of bright green grass which stretched out down to a sparkling pool.

'This place is like a resort!' Mae said, shaking her head.

We quickly pulled on our training leotards – none of us had brought swimmers to school that day, but our leotards were fine for a swim.

Evie tossed a towel to each one of us. 'Well, what are we waiting for?' she grinned.

We ran out to the pool. Evie charged forwards and did a somersault into the water. The rest of us gave one look to each other and squealed as we followed her in.

'So, what's the plan for keeping Bella out of the top-twelve in the comp?' Evie said as she lazily swam about the pool.

'I reckon we just need to keep her out of the top rankings in every apparatus,' Mae said. 'If we can each beat her on at least one apparatus, then she's not going to do that well overall.'

'Yeah, and we are all good at different things anyhow,' said Anwen, lying on her tummy by the side of the pool, drying herself off in the afternoon sun. 'Abby, you can nail floor, Evie, vault, I'm okay on beam and Mae has a gorgeous bar routine.'

'But Bella's routines have such a high level of difficulty.' Mae frowned.

The gymnastics scoring had changed since the London Olympics, and gymnasts were now rewarded for difficulty as well as nailing a clean routine. When I first started gymnastics, the scores were just out of ten. You started with ten and points were slowly taken away for each mistake you made. But now there were two scores. There was the score for the compulsory parts of the routine, but you could add on bonus points for making the skills more difficult. So theoretically, there was no limit to the score you could achieve.

'I reckon the only way to beat her is if we all up our difficulty,' Evie said. 'We each need to add an extra skill on our best apparatus to make sure we beat her. I'm going to work on adding some twists to my Tsuk on vault.'

'I'll add a release on my bar routine,' said Mae.

'Argh, that means I need to stick a layout on beam.' Anwen sighed. 'Freaks me out.'

'And I'll up the ante on my last tumbling row,' I said nervously. I just hoped I could actually do it.

'Awesome!' Evie laughed. 'With elements like those, she'll never beat us.'

'Enjoying your little mothers' meeting?' a teasing voice said from behind us. We all spun around to see Evie's brother Andy wandering down to the pool.

Andy had dark brown hair which matched his big chocolate brown eyes. He was tall with olive skin and wide-set shoulders. Evie had told us that he was a rugby player in Year 9 at the Academy of Sport for Boys. That's the 'brother school' of the girls' Academy.

Andy took a running jump and did a huge bomb into the pool, splashing us as we stood on the side. He got out of the pool and wandered over in our direction.

'Oh, sorry, I didn't even introduce myself,' Andy said. 'I'm Andy.'

'Mae.'

'A-A-Abby,' I stammered.

Andy held out both his hands at the same time to shake ours. Mae and I reached out and grasped his large hands, shaking them politely. I could feel my face reddening. I'm sure it was just the sun. Suddenly Andy yanked us both, sending me and Mae flying into the pool. I gasped as I broke the surface of the water, only to see Andy laughing hysterically.

'Nice to meet you!' He chuckled as he headed over to the sun lounges on the other side of the pool.

Suddenly, there was a melodic beeping noise sounding from the cabana.

'Coming!' Evie yelled as she wrapped a towel around her waist. She trotted over to the side of the cabana where an intercom system was hooked up to the wall. 'Yes, Mum?' she asked as she pressed the button. Evie's mum's voice crackled through the intercom.

'Abby's mum is here, darling.'

'Oh, that's me,' I said as I grabbed my towel. The others slipped their towels on too and followed me out the pool gate. I glanced back as I started to walk up the grassed lawn. Andy looked at me over his sunnies and gently winked and smiled. I felt my stomach drop to the floor. That was a new feeling. I quickly spun back to face the house and raced up the lawn as fast as I could.

# CHAPTER *Six*

'So what is $x + y$? Anyone? Abby?'

I jumped as Mr Dory called my name.

'Oh. Um, $x + y$ … um …' I stared down at my textbook, begging it to telepathically send me the answer. 'XY?'

'No, Abby, we just went through this. Watch again.' Mr Dory glided his stylus along the smartboard.

'$x + y = x + y$. And $x$ x $y = xy$. See?'

I turned to my new friend sitting next to me, Ava. Ava was a swimmer at the Academy and we had found ourselves together in Science, Maths and History. Ava gave a confused shrug as the bell pierced through the loudspeakers.

'Everyone, complete the exercises on page one hundred and thirteen for homework and we'll go through more of this tomorrow,' Mr Dory yelled over the rustle of books closing.

Ava slapped her textbook shut with a bang. 'Argh, could that period have gone on any longer? Torture.'

I gathered my books and hugged them to my chest as we walked out the door.

'I've gotta run – training starts now. See you tomorrow, Abby!' Ava yelled as she jogged away with her swimming bag bouncing around on her side. The corridor was its usual hive of activity – hockey sticks ramming me in the arm, girls gathering their tennis rackets and soccer balls and some girls slipping on their jodhpurs right there in the hallway. We'd had a full day of classes and lots of people had after school training. For sports girls, sitting in a classroom all day is like torture – especially when you're not used to it. We were accustomed to running around, swimming, riding, or in my case, flying. It was like being stuck in a cage sitting through a double period of Maths.

I wandered over to my locker where Evie, Anwen and Mae were collecting their gear. The other students disappeared quickly, not wanting to be late for after school training. Our coaches were in a meeting so we had half an hour to kill before training started.

'I'm starving,' moaned Evie.

I fished around my backpack and pulled out my lunch box. I popped the lid off only to find some crusts and an apple core.

'I need FOOOOOD!' whinged Evie.

'We could quickly run down to the shops,' offered Anwen.

Mae frowned. 'We only have half an hour – we'll never make it back.'

We slumped down onto the corridor floor and settled for our drink bottles and a pack of sultanas that Anwen had found in her bag.

'So, you're hungry?' a voice said from beside us. We looked up to see Scarlet Belyakov standing by her locker. 'I know where we can get some food,' she said, the corners of her mouth curled into a mischievous smile. We looked at each other a little confused. We hadn't spoken to Scarlet since she'd stormed off on the morning of my birthday. 'Well, you coming?' she asked in her usual husky voice. Evie shrugged and we stood up slowly, following Scarlet down the hallway.

Scarlet led us through the grounds of the school, down the pathway and past the tuckshop which had its shutters locked tight. We curved up the grassy hill towards the school office. Maintenance men clipped the hedges and pruned the roses. Cleaning staff began to fill the corridors, sweeping down the concrete and blowing the leaves away with leaf blowers. It really was an impeccably kept school.

'Where exactly are we going?' asked Anwen.

'Trust me,' Scarlet said as she walked on.

We reached the office and Scarlet turned to us. 'Right. I need you to go around to the other side of the office, on the reading lawn. I want you to line up, and when you hear the music, start tumbling.'

'What?' I blurted out.

'Start tumbling. It's grass – you'll be fine. Have fun with it.'

'What music?' we said in unison.

'You'll see,' Scarlet smiled.

Evie, Mae, Anwen and I walked around the office, curiously peering in the window to see what Scarlet was doing. She walked through the office door and approached the desk. She asked the secretary on the front desk something and the secretary nodded and disappeared into the back room. As she did, Scarlet jumped over the desk and yanked her iPod out of her pocket. She whizzed her finger around the controls and leant it against the intercom microphone. She then hit a switch. Music began to blare through the outdoor intercom speakers. The other school secretaries inside didn't seem to notice, so the music mustn't have been coming through the internal speakers.

As soon as the music started, we sprung to life. Mae began by walking the length of the grass on her hands. A few hockey students passing by stopped to look. Evie was next – she launched into a quick round-off and punched out two flips. The hockey players started to cheer. A few girls with riding helmets paused to watch. Anwen then did a whole row of front walkovers, each walkover getting a louder cheer from the ever-growing crowd. I glanced up and saw the office secretaries stand and look curiously out the window. One of them motioned for the others to come and look too.

They all leant up to the windows, craning to see the spectacle on the grass.

It was my turn. I punched out a round-off and added two flips and a sommie. The crowd erupted in cheers. Even the secretaries were clapping from the window, laughing and throwing their hands in the air.

All of a sudden, a loud voice was heard over the music. 'Where is this music coming from?' It was Mrs Brunette, the principal. Immediately, Evie, Anwen, Mae and I stopped tumbling and disappeared into the crowd. The crowd cheered loudly, enjoying the after school show. Mrs Brunette looked at the intercom speakers and frowned. She briskly walked up the stairs to the office and flung open the doors. We could see from our hiding place in the crowd that Mrs Brunette was speaking angrily to the secretaries. They jumped to their feet and hurriedly found the iPod which was leaning against the microphone, unbeknownst to them. The music stopped abruptly. The crowd dissipated and we crouched down by a nearby bush, wildly looking around for Scarlet. Was she still in the office? Was she in trouble?

'What are you looking at?'

'AAAAH!' We all jumped out of our skin.

'What the heck, Scarlet?' Evie yelled. 'You trying to give us heart attacks?'

Scarlet smiled and put her hands in her pockets. She pulled out a massive stack of biscuits, which she held out for us to take.

'Where'd you get those?' Mae cried.

'The office, of course,' Scarlet replied, tossing the biscuits to each of us. 'They have a whole jar in there. Thanks for creating the diversion.'

'I can't believe I was an accomplice to a crime and I didn't even know it!' Anwen said, wide-eyed.

Evie chortled loudly and took a biscuit. Mae and I shrugged and joined in eating

Scarlet's loot. After a minute or two, even Anwen started munching on the biscuits.

'What about your iPod?' Mae asked Scarlet.

'Ah, that's okay. I'll sneak in tomorrow and get it back. They'll never know it's mine.'

We finished devouring the stack of biscuits that Scarlet had stolen from the office. 'Man, next time remind me to take more,' she said, wiping her mouth casually.

'Next time?' Anwen said with a worried frown.

'Yeah, next time. I left them a note, you see,' Scarlet replied. 'I slipped it into the empty jar when I cleaned them out of their boring biscuits.'

'You didn't dob us in, did you?' I asked, horrified.

Scarlet smiled. 'Nah. I just wrote "Next time, choc chip, please".'

We looked at each other and burst out laughing. We rolled down onto the grass and laughed and laughed until our sides hurt.

That afternoon, Scarlet ended up training with our group. We were focusing on bars and I was trying to really concentrate – bars wasn't my best apparatus and I needed to nail it for the competition. I was working on my dismount which was a double back somersault off the bars. Every time I tried, I'd land short and have to put my hands on the mat. After the tenth try, I jumped to the ground, frustrated and exhausted.

'Get a drink, Abs,' Coach Rebecca said, letting me off the hook.

'You know how I get a double rotation in?' a cool voice said from behind me. I turned to see Bella standing over me, her hand on one hip. 'I let go just a bit earlier so that I have more time to finish the turns. Chuck your head back a bit too for more oomph.'

I frowned. That didn't sound quite right. But it could be worth a shot. I nodded quickly in thanks. Bella smirked.

I jumped up and dusted some chalk onto my grips. I clapped my hands, sending a puff of chalk into the air. I did a quick glide kip to get up to the low bar and then jumped my feet onto the bar so I was standing. I launched my arms out and leapt to the high bar, doing another kip to get my hips up. I did a big cast, kicking my legs as high to handstand as they would go. Then I began swinging around the bar in a series of giants, preparing for my dismount. After the last giant, I swung down, ready to release. I let go of the bar earlier than I usually would and chucked my head back. It felt really weird. I realised I was way too low and I only got halfway around my second somersault. I landed hard on my hands and knees. My whole body ached. I looked up and saw Bella snicker.

'Abby, you released way too early,' Coach Rebecca said, helping me to my feet. 'And you chucked your head back. You'll never get in a double sommie that way. You're lucky you didn't break an arm!'

I scowled at Bella as I walked back to my friends. I couldn't work out why Bella had it in for me, but she clearly didn't like me. I had a suspicion that it was because she thought I didn't belong at the Academy.

'Nice stack, Abs,' smiled Evie. 'You okay?'

'Yeah,' I replied, still scowling at Bella. 'Remind me never to take advice from Bella again,' I said, rubbing my elbow.

'Bella told you to do that?' Anwen asked, alarmed. 'That's so dangerous!'

'Don't worry, Abby, we'll get her back with our competition plan,' Mae said, comforting me.

'So what's the plan to dethrone Queen Bella?' a husky voice said from beside us. It was Scarlet. We all looked alarmed. 'Don't worry,

I'm not going to spill your secret. So what are you gonna do? Tamper with her hand grips? Hit her legs with a cricket bat?'

Anwen gasped, mortified.

Scarlet laughed. 'I'm kidding.'

'We're just planning to increase our skill values on one apparatus. If each of us can win one apparatus, then hopefully we'll all get through to the final team, which we hope would spoil Bella's chances of getting in,' Mae explained. Scarlet nodded, thinking.

Suddenly there was a gasp from a group of girls on beam. 'Look!' one of them shrieked. 'It's Katherine Belyakov!' All the girls looked up in awe, craning their necks to catch a glimpse of one of the best Olympic gymnasts to ever come out of the country.

'I wonder if she'll sign an autograph!' one of them squealed. The girls rushed to the glass doors to have a look at Katherine, standing in the foyer. Scarlet frowned, her cheeks reddening. Her eyes were burning with anger as she stared in the direction of her famous sister.

The doors opened and Katherine tiptoed in, trying to be inconspicuous.

'Can you sign my diary?' one of the gymnasts said, running to get a pen from her bag. Katherine was clearly embarrassed.

Scarlet grabbed her drink bottle and stormed over to her sister. 'Why are you here? I told you not to come to my school!'

'Scarlet, I had to pick you up early – Mum's car has broken down – I'm sorry but –'

'Save it!' Scarlet hissed. She stormed out the door and slammed it behind her. Katherine shook her head sadly as a group of gymnasts gathered around her. They shot questions at her about her time in the Olympics, vying for her attention. Katherine meekly waved to them and trotted out the door after her sister.

'That was a bit weird,' Mae said. 'Katherine was just picking Scarlet up. Why does she have to explode all the time?'

'She scares me!' whispered Anwen. 'One minute she's funny and kind and then next she's cold and angry.'

'I think we should just keep our distance from Scarlet. She's too volatile,' I said. It pained me to say it – I really felt like we'd had a good afternoon with her – but with a temper like that I thought we'd be better off just staying away. The others nodded in agreement.

# CHAPTER *Seven*

*Bling!*

I jumped up to the computer as my messenger alert went off.

*Evie: How sore are your quads from those leaping drills?*

I giggled.

*Abby: In agony.*

*Evie: Can't believe Bella set you up like that today.*

*Abby: I've got a nice bruise on my hip to prove it. What's her problem?!*

*Evie: She's jealous because we are bosses.*

*Abby: Reckon?! ;)*

*Evie: Totes. We'll get her back tho. Wait till the comp when we wipe the floor with her. We'll all make the squad and she'll be left hanging out with everyone else who didn't get in. Woohoo!*

*Abby: That'd be awesome. Better go. Speaking of agony, I have to finish that algebra homework.*

*Evie: See ya tomoz! x*

I smiled as I closed the messenger window and got up from the computer. I walked back to my room from the family room and sat at my desk, my algebra homework glaring at me. The letters and numbers may as well have been in another language – it was completely over my head. I began to hum the tune to my new floor routine I'd been working on since joining the Academy. I tapped my pencil lightly on the paper in front of me.

*Split leap, side leap, pose …*

I shook my head and tried to focus on my Maths homework. The music in my mind became louder.

*Ooh!* I jumped up. I'd thought of a great new pose to finish my series of leaps. I stood in front of the mirror and practised it. Nice. I tried it again, keeping my chin up.

'Working hard then?'

I was startled by the voice at my door. 'Dad, you freaked me out.'

'What happened to Maths?' he asked, raising one eyebrow.

'I was doing it,' I said quickly as I leapt back to my desk chair. 'But I just got this idea for a pose and …' I trailed off as I saw that his unimpressed expression hadn't changed at all.

'Sit,' he said sternly. 'Remember, school first.'

I nodded. One of the conditions of starting at the Academy was that I wouldn't fall behind in my schoolwork just because I was in a sports school. Dad wandered towards me and peered over my shoulder.

'Algebra, hey?'

I groaned.

'Need some help?'

I looked up hopefully and nodded. Dad pulled up a footstool and sat next to me. I smiled. Dad patiently took me through the chapter, making me practise the sums over and over. I guess if you think about it, it's not that different to doing a gymnastics drill. Sometimes in the gym we can do the same movement 1000 times, making sure we get it right every time. It feels really boring, especially when it's something easy. I remember once we had to stand on the beam and gently rise onto the balls of our feet. We repeated this simple movement, up and down, for over an hour. We were trying to get to 100 lifts, but every time someone fell off the beam or wobbled, we'd start again. It was one of the most tedious drills of my life, but when I jumped back on the beam the next day, I felt 100 per cent more stable as I walked along it.

That night I couldn't sleep. I lay in bed and shut my eyes but I couldn't stop thinking about what had happened at training. Bella really was starting to get in my head. Why was she trying to sabotage me? Was it because she thought I didn't deserve to be in the Academy? I sighed and tried to push that thought to the back of my mind, but deep down I had a terrible feeling that maybe she was right.

# CHAPTER *Eight*

'Can I have one?'

'Argh, yes, just one,' Evie said, irritated. She handed over a hot chip to one of the other gymnasts who took the salty chip gratefully.

It was another afternoon where we had half an hour to kill before our training session. Evie's mum had texted her saying she was nearby and asked if we wanted some afternoon tea delivered. Evie practically screamed with excitement, texting her mum back and asking for the mother lode of hot chips for us. But sure enough, the second it arrived, it seemed every student in the school could smell the fatty goodness of the chips and wanted in on the action.

'We need to hide!' Mae laughed.

'I know a spot,' a voice said from behind us. We looked up and saw Scarlet standing by her locker. We glanced awkwardly at each other. We hadn't spoken to Scarlet since her little meltdown in the gym. We had vowed to avoid her – she was clearly trouble. We looked around, trying to avoid her eye contact.

'Oh, come on,' she smiled, 'I'm not the devil!'

'Ooh, can I have a chip?' asked a random girl. Evie reluctantly parted with another hot chip as she began to stand up.

'Show us the way,' Evie said flatly to Scarlet.

Scarlet led us along the school corridor. We passed classroom after classroom, all empty of students. The hallways were pretty dead too as most sports had begun afternoon training. We reached a row of lockers which belonged to some of the older students. Next to them was a three-tiered wooden bag rack, which usually held all their school and sports bags. Scarlet began to yank the bag rack, slowly moving it to the other side of the hallway.

'A little help?' she groaned.

We looked at each other, confused, but shrugged our shoulders and helped her push the rack to the other side of the hall. Scarlet then scaled the bag rack, climbing to the top shelf. She stood tall on top of the rack, and gently pushed open a hatch in the ceiling.

'What are you waiting for?' she asked as she hauled herself up into the roof cavity.

'I don't know about this,' Anwen stammered.

But before we could object, Evie had already pulled herself into the roof space, taking the steaming hot chips with her. Mae quickly followed, then I jumped up, followed by a nervous Anwen.

It was quite dark in the roof space, but light enough with the hatch open. It smelled musty and I wrinkled my nose which itched from the dust. We sat in a circle, being careful not to bump our heads on the wooden beams which crisscrossed above us. A bit of graffiti on one of the beams betrayed the secret of someone else's hiding spot from years gone by. Each of us picked at the pile of chips in the middle.

'Aah, no interruptions!' smiled Evie as she popped another chip into her mouth.

'I'm a bit scared,' said Anwen. 'I mean, what if someone lives up here – someone crazy! Like Bertha in the attic in *Jane Eyre*!'

'What are you talking about?' laughed Evie.

'*Jane Eyre* – it's our English text this term Evie, *remember?*'

'Ah. Mental note: read *Jane Eyre*.'

'So, tell me more about this plan to oust Bella from Squad A,' Scarlet said, shaking her head and smiling.

We all glanced nervously at each other.

'What?' Scarlet asked, sensing our reluctance to include her in our plan.

'Okay, look,' said Evie, breaking the tension. If anyone was going to address the elephant in the room (or attic) it was going to be Evie. She was as subtle as a sledgehammer. 'We like you, Scarlet. But one minute you are setting up elaborate plans to feed us stolen biscuits and laughing with us on the lawn and the next second you are all crazy ape-woman, slamming doors and storming off. What gives?'

Even in the dim roof space we could see Scarlet's face redden. She looked to the floor and frowned in silence.

'Is it us? Do we make you nervous? Why did you sit down for cake with us the other week then storm off? It doesn't make sense,' Mae said.

'It's . . . it's not you guys,' Scarlet stammered. 'It's . . . I dunno, I guess I'm just sick of it.'

'Sick of what?' Anwen asked gently. 'Sick of gym? Do you feel forced into being here?'

Scarlet looked up sharply. 'What? No! I love gym. It's the only time where I feel free and happy and confident.'

'Then what is it?' I asked, shaking my head lightly in confusion.

'It's Katherine. My sister, Katherine! That day I sat with you guys on Abby's birthday – the first thing you did was start asking about my sister. And the first day we came to this school, I saw the whispers when I said my surname. How do you think it feels being the sister of the famous Katherine Belyakov? She's an Olympic champion! No gymnast wants to be *my* friend, they just want to know about my famous sister! And then she walked into the gym. Into *my* gym. This is where I train – this is *my* home. And she walks in the door and everyone runs over for autographs! I told her never to come here. How do you think it makes me feel?'

By now Scarlet's eyes were damp with tears. She wiped them away aggressively and took a deep breath. She'd obviously been holding that in for a really long time. Suddenly, her long dark hair and dark eyes were not mysterious and menacing, but vulnerable and sad. Anwen put her hand gently on Scarlet's leg.

'That must be tough – I'm sorry I never thought about it that way,' Anwen said quietly. Scarlet sniffed and smiled.

'Well, that's easy,' said Evie after a pause. 'We just won't talk about your sister anymore. To us you are just plain old Scarlet … no Belyakov!'

'Really? It's that simple?' Scarlet said incredulously.

'Yep, that simple,' I said. 'You hang with us and we won't talk about your sister. Promise.'

Scarlet smiled the warmest smile I'd ever seen on her face.

'And you do realise this means you need to make it to Squad A with us, and help us dethrone Queen Bella,' Mae said with her eyebrows raised.

'It's a deal,' laughed Scarlet. 'I'm going to increase my difficulty on my last tumbling row on floor.'

'Oh, good!' said Evie. 'That way the pressure is off Abby on floor too!'

*What was THAT supposed to mean?* I thought.

The hot chips were well and truly obliterated by this stage, so Evie scrunched up the empty paper and crawled to the hole in the roof to get down.

'Um, guys?' she said warily.

We huddled around the manhole to look below. To our horror, the bag rack had been moved!

'How are we going to get down?' Anwen shrieked. The drop to the ground was pretty high and none of us were game enough to risk a broken ankle.

Suddenly, we heard the swishing of a broom along the concrete. It was Mr Thomas, one of

the school maintenance staff. He must have moved the bag rack while we were in the roof. He was a lovely old man with greying hair and kind eyes.

'Um, Mr Thomas?' Evie called from the roof space.

Mr Thomas looked around, confused as to where the noise was coming from. Then he looked up to see five pairs of eyes staring at him from the ceiling.

'Oh my! What are you girls doing?' he called with an alarmed expression on his face.

'Er, just looking,' ventured Evie. Scarlet snorted with laughter at Evie's lame excuse. Mr Thomas chuckled to himself and began to push the bag rack back underneath the hole.

'Come on, then, before someone sees you!' he said.

We each climbed down, trying very hard to hide the smiles on our faces.

'Naughty, naughty girls,' he kept muttering as we bolted down the corridor, squealing with laughter.

‘I’d like to change my last tumbling row,’ I said, trying to sound confident. Coach Ana raised an eyebrow. ‘I want to keep my double back somersault but add a full twist.’

‘Erm, right. That’s interesting, Abby, why?’

‘I just … I think upping my difficulty will get me a better score in the competition,’ I said, trying to hold the waver in my voice.

‘Yes,’ Coach Ana said slowly, ‘but doing it badly will ruin your score. It’s not just about chucking in the hardest tumbling skills you can. You have to do them *well*.’

‘I can do it, I know I can. Can I at least try? Please?’

Coach Ana stood, thinking hard. Finally she nodded. ‘Okay, start by tumbling into the pit. I want a soft landing for you if you are trying a new skill. But remember, Abby, the comp is in a week – you have almost no time to nail this. But I'll let you try.'

I squealed lightly and ran down the mats which led to the tumbling pit. I started some basic tumbles to warm up, then launched into my ordinary final tumbling row, in tuck position. I could do it perfectly.

'Okay, twist time!' called Ana from the pit-end of the mats. 'Go!'

I pumped my arms with all my might. I launched into a strong round-off then punched out a long, fierce flip. I needed serious momentum. I started to soar in the air. I then pulled my arms in to get myself twisting. I landed in the soft foam cubes, with my face muffled in the foam. If that had been on the mats, I probably would have broken my nose.

'You don't have the height,' Coach Ana explained. 'That's why you don't have enough time to complete the rotation. You need more height and a faster turn. Are you sure this is what you want, Abby?'

I nodded, determined. I'd promised the girls I'd increase the difficulty on my best apparatus, which was floor. If we all dominated our best apparatus, then Bella had less chance of placing on each one. And I had to prove to the others that I didn't need Scarlet to help get Bella out of the medals for floor. I was just as good as anyone else there, wasn't I? I had to do this. Not just for me, but for my friends.

The afternoon ticked on into early evening. Slowly, each of the girls began to warm down and head to the change rooms. But I was still working on my tumbling. When I looked up, I suddenly realised there was hardly anyone left in the gym. Coach Rebecca had told me to warm down and go home several times, but I'd kept saying 'just one more'.

I pumped my arms, my feet feeling like lead. I grimaced as I punched out my flip and tried to get the height for the twisting double somersaults. But I was exhausted. I landed in the pit on my back, panting heavily. I tried to sit up, but fell back down, too exhausted to climb through the foam cubes.

'Need a hand?' a voice said from above. I looked up to see Mae's smiling face.

'What are you still doing here?'

'I just changed to go home and noticed your bag in the change rooms. Here,' she held out her hand and yanked me out of the pit. 'You're going to burn out working that hard, Abby,' she said, frowning. 'You know tomorrow we need to turn up again for a whole other session. Leave something in the tank!'

I smiled and linked arms with her. To be honest, I think I needed her just to get me back to the change rooms I was so tired.

'I just really want to get this,' I said, sighing. 'We are all depending on each other.'

'Abby, you can't carry the weight of everyone else on your shoulders. Sure, we have a plan to keep Bella out, but it's not just down to you.'

'I just don't want to disappoint everyone.'

'That's great, Abby, but don't compromise on yourself,' Mae said wisely. 'Don't compromise your own comp and don't compromise who you are.'

I smiled at my new friend. We'd only been together at school for a matter of weeks and already I felt like I had the best friends in the whole world.

'Come on, let's get to the train station,' Mae said, picking up my bag for me.

# CHAPTER *Nine*

The next week went by in a blur. During training sessions tensions were running high. Everyone was full of nerves with the upcoming competition looming closer. It seemed like Bella was more intent than ever on sabotaging me. As her routines became cleaner and better each day, her mean remarks filled me with self-doubt. She clearly thought I didn't deserve to be at the Academy and she wasn't going to stop until everyone knew it.

Everyone trained hard, trying to get their routines perfect for the competition. Evie had successfully added a twist to her vault. She was such a powerful gymnast and I admit, I was jealous at how quickly she could master a new skill. Anwen had to face her fears and add a layout to her tumbling row on beam. Mae added a release to her bar routine. This wasn't hard for her because she'd had the release in her routine previously, but took it out before the last competition because it wasn't perfect. But with the extra few weeks at the Academy, she was able to add it back in. And Scarlet, who seemed to be able to do any skill she tried, had increased the difficulty on her floor routine like it was the simplest thing in the world. So there was just me. I really didn't want to let everyone down by not adding a new, more difficult element to my routine. But my double twisting somersault in my last tumbling row was not looking good. I never had the height off the ground to land it cleanly. Most of the time I'd land on my knees or sometimes with my entire face in the mat. Coach Ana really wanted me to take it out. She knew I could nail the double somersault without a twist and she thought I'd get a much better score keeping it that way. *But if I could do the harder skill and nail it …*

The competition was being held in the Academy gym. Coach Ana had invited some judges along to help score the competition and parents were allowed to view from the gallery above.

The change room was buzzing with nervous chatter. A thick cloud of hairspray surrounded us all.

'Can you do mine now?' Mae asked. I nodded as I sprayed the hairspray onto her bottom. I know, sounds totally weird, right? But a little hairspray on the bottom of the leotard stopped it riding up and giving you an embarrassing wedgie. Not to mention you lose points if your undies show!

Slowly, we began to pull our leotards on. I couldn't believe the difference. Evie, Mae, Anwen, Scarlet and I stood side by side, looking at ourselves in the long mirrors across the wall of basins. The blue and white leotards shone under the halogen lights of the change room. All of us had our hair pulled back into tight buns with a sparkly silver scrunchie to match the beads on our leotards. The light caught the sparkle in our hairspray, making a shimmering halo around us. We stood in silence.

'Well, I guess this is it,' said Mae. 'Our first comp as Academy gymnasts.'

We held hands as we stood in front of the mirror.

'Right, let's do this!' Evie yelled, shattering the silence between us. We broke into wide grins and began to make our way upstairs to the gym.

As we entered the gym, it was like a totally different place to where we trained. Everything was neat and tidy for the competition. Long tables stood in front of each apparatus – the judges' tables. Electronic score cards stood on top of tall stands, guarding each apparatus. The score cards would light up each score in bright red – there was nowhere to hide. They would reveal scores of exhilaration and scores of devastation, all without prejudice.

The usual mess of chalk covering the bar mats, vault run and even on the floor mats had been meticulously cleaned away. I suddenly felt a sickening feeling as I stared at the floor mats. What was going to happen in my last tumbling row?

The judges entered the gymnasium, they were wearing smart navy blue suits and skirts with white shirts. They looked so serious. Coach Ana's voice boomed over the loudspeaker as she spoke into the microphone.

'Would all gymnasts please line up on the mats so we can get the competition underway.'

Nervous girls tiptoed over to the mats,

making final adjustments to their hair and leotards.

'Now,' Coach Ana continued, 'we will be rotating around the apparatus in our training groups.'

Evie squealed. This meant that Mae, Evie, Anwen and I would be in the same group. Oh, and Bella. Scarlet pulled a sad face as she realised she wouldn't be with us. Anwen patted her back affectionately.

'Training group one will start on bars. Training group two on beam, three on vault and four on floor.'

Okay, so that meant we would start on bars. It also meant floor would be last. I couldn't work out if this was good or bad – it meant that I would be thinking about my tumbling row for the entire competition. But it also meant I didn't have to face it just yet.

Our group stood up silently and walked in unison over to the bars, stopping in front of the judges' table.

'Welcome, girls,' the head judge said. We smiled nervously.

'First up will be Evie Brown, then Mae Choon, Isabella Burnetti, Anwen Jones, Abigail Rogers, Claudia Cox, Sophie Bell. You get one warm-up each.'

We nodded and turned to sit on the bench to strap on our hand grips. Evie went straight to the chalk bucket and proceeded to run through her routine. Each of us quickly ran through our own routines as well. Some girls left off their dismount, worrying about injuring themselves before the comp. Others ran through the routine as if it were the real thing. With Mae's added release, Coach Rebecca stood under the bars to spot her if she needed it. She was attempting the hardest skill of us all and having her there gave her added confidence. Coach Rebecca was even allowed to stand under Mae to catch her in the real competition, but she was not allowed to touch her without the judges taking off points.

After running through our routines, the competition began. Music blared through the speakers as one of the other groups began their floor routines. My stomach sank as I thought about it.

Evie started the competition for us. She glided through her bar routine in beautiful, fluid swings. Her long, tanned legs flew gracefully through the air as she nailed each and every element of her routine. She wound up in a series of giant swings and landed with her feet together on the mat below, only taking a tiny hop forwards. She presented to the judges and we all cheered.

The judges scribbled in a frenzied manner and leant in to compare scores. You'd think gymnastics judging is based on whether they like your routine or not, right? Well, funnily enough it's not. Each mistake has a set penalty. Each element has a set degree of difficulty. One little hop would deduct 0.1 off your score. A fall, more. So even though there were four different judges, most of the time the scores came in with only one tenth of a point difference between them. Pretty incredible, really.

The red electronic score card lit up. 12.85. Evie beamed. It was a great score, particularly since it wasn't the hardest routine. But Evie had nailed the execution.

Next was Mae's turn. This was her big moment on her best apparatus.

'Go, Mae!' we all cheered in unison.

Mae's routine began smoothly. She flew around the bar, jumping onto the low bar and soaring through the air to the high bar. Her giants were long and beautiful. But then it was time for her big release. Coach Rebecca stood underneath the bars in case Mae fell. Mae released the bar and soared through the air down to the low bar, catching it with perfect precision. Coach Rebecca stepped away from the bars, smiling as Mae continued with her routine. Every element seemed perfect, all the way through to her perfect landing. We cheered loudly as she presented to the judges.

The judges conferred.

The electronic score card lit up 13.10! It was an awesome score, with Mae clearly being rewarded for her risky releases and technical moves. Mae hugged me tightly as she saw her score. I glanced over and saw Bella swallowing hard. I think she was realising that this competition was not going to be as easy as she may have thought.

Bella's routine was clean, and we watched, slightly annoyed, as she breezed through move after move. Bella started to wind up her giants for her dismount. It wasn't a particularly difficult dismount, so she usually completed it with ease. But as Bella hit the mats hard, she let out a slight yelp. She remained on her feet and produced a tight smile and presented to the judges. But as she walked off the mats, she was limping.

She sat down, clearly choking back tears. Coach Rebecca went to her immediately and began inspecting her foot, gently rotating it round and round. As she did, light tears pricked Bella's eyes.

'I'm okay, it was just a weird landing,' she said in a wavering voice.

Anwen and I both pumped out solid bar routines to add to the mix. Neither of us were strong bar workers, so our routines lacked difficulty. But neither of us fell off and we both stuck our landings. Anwen came in with a 12.5 and I scored a 12.8. Solid.

Our next rotation was beam. Poor Anwen looked terrified, she was so nervous. This was the apparatus where she'd increased her difficulty and added a layout. A layout is like a somersault, but your body is straight instead of tucked up. It requires a lot of height and is very difficult on beam.

Anwen gracefully mounted the beam. Her tiny little arms moved around in dance motions. Her leap series was beautiful – high off the beam and confident. She then had to do a sheep jump followed by a backflip. This is called a connection. It means that you can't stop in between the two movements otherwise you don't get your bonus points. A sheep jump is hard enough – Anwen had to jump up and throw her head backwards while she flicked her toes back towards her head. It meant she could not see the beam at all in that moment. Anwen jumped high and did a beautiful sheep jump, but as she landed, she wobbled slightly. As she recovered from the wobble, she added in the backflip.

'I don't think they're going to award her the connection,' sighed Evie. I nodded.

Anwen took a deep breath as she stood up at the end of the beam. She was clearly psyching herself up for the big layout. She took a couple of strong steps and punched out a round-off, followed by a soaring layout. Her feet hit the beam hard in unison. She smiled brightly as we all gave a quiet cheer.

Anwen ended the routine with a solid backward layout to the ground. She presented to the judges with her cute little smile and trotted back over to us.

'Argh, if only I didn't pause in my connection,' she said, frustrated.

'But you nailed the layout! Awesome!' Evie said, giving her a supportive hug.

Suddenly I felt a tap on my shoulder.

'Where's Coach Rebecca?' Bella asked.

'I think she's gone to the other group for this round,' I answered.

I could tell Bella was worried. She bit her lip and looked around wildly.

'Are … are you okay?' I asked.

'I just need to know something for my routine. My ankle still hurts and I want to rest it as much as possible before vault and floor. If I swap out my back somersault for a simple backflip, then I won't put as much strain on it. But I don't know if the somersault is a compulsory element.'

A compulsory element means that you have to include that element in your routine. I knew for a fact that a back tumbling element was compulsory, but it had to involve no hands. A backflip would mean that Bella's hands would touch the beam and she wouldn't be awarded it. I frowned, thinking. If Bella left off the compulsory element, it would hit her score hard. I thought about how she tricked me at training into falling off bars. I thought about how mean she was to everyone around her.

'A backflip is fine – it's not compulsory to do a sommie,' I said quickly.

'Thanks, Abby,' she smiled gratefully.

I felt terrible. As Bella took a sip from her water bottle and got ready to do her routine, I felt like I had swallowed a brick. I looked over to my friends who were huddled together, smiling happily as they congratulated Anwen on her routine. Surely they'd be happy that I was keeping Bella out of the top twelve, wouldn't they?

'Isabella Burnetti,' the head judge said.

I didn't have time to ask my friends what they thought. Bella stood tall and shook out her arms.

Suddenly, Mae's words from the week before echoed through my mind. She said it wasn't my responsibility to get everyone into the top twelve. And she said I should never compromise who I am. But who am I? A cheat? A sabotage? But Bella had been so mean to me.

Bella stepped onto the mat.

'Wait!' I whispered, pulling her arm.

'Abby, get off me, it's my turn!' she hissed.

'Bella, you have to do the sommie, it's compulsory,' I blurted out.

'Isabella Burnetti, are you ready?' called the judge.

Bella looked at me and narrowed her eyes. I could see confusion in her face. Maybe she thought I was trying to hurt her ankle more. Maybe she thought I was lying now.

'Bella, it's true, trust me,' I pleaded. Bella turned to the beam as I let go of her arm.

*Oh, please believe me!*

Bella did a gentle mount, obviously trying to save her ankle the pain. Her routine was not as solid as it usually was. She seemed rattled. She completed each leap with a slight wince which betrayed her secret pain. Then came her final tumbling row. Bella stood at the end of the beam and took a breath. For a split second she glanced in my direction. I lifted my eyebrows and nodded. *Believe me*.

Bella launched into a strong round-off. Was she going to do a flip or a somersault? I held my breath. I heard her groan slightly as she pushed out of the round-off and into a soaring back somersault, which she landed with precision.

'Yes!' I couldn't help blurting out. My friends looked over at me, confused.

Bella completed a tidy dismount and presented to the judges. Then she limped over to the rest of us. At that moment, Coach Rebecca came back over.

'Nice work!' she smiled at Bella. 'Look,' she said, pointing to the scoreboard. '12.9. Really solid, Bella,' she smiled.

'Coach, is a somersault compulsory?' Bella asked, raising her eyebrows at me. 'I was going to do a flip to save my ankle.'

'Well thank goodness you didn't,' said Coach Rebecca. 'You need a no-handed back tumble. You would have really ruined your comp if you'd done that!'

Bella's eyes widened, incredulous. She opened her mouth to say something, but then shut it again. I nodded at her briefly and then took my place, ready for my beam routine.

When my name was called, I tiptoed onto the spongy blue mat and presented to the judges with a nervous smile. They stared back at me, emotionless, with their pencils poised to note down every error I might make. I mounted the beam with steadiness and stood tall and straight, focused. I began my routine with a series of leaps. My leaps were high and graceful and I landed each one solidly. Next came a connection. I did a neat backflip and added a layout which I stepped out of one foot at a time. I stuck it neatly and smiled.

I went through a series of other dance moves, plus a 'close to beam' movement. This meant that my body had to touch the beam – not just my feet or hands, but my stomach or back. I stood up and continued through a series of leaps and static skills. I could feel myself approaching the end of the routine – and I hadn't fallen off! All I had left was my dismount. I breathed out heavily as I focused down to the end of the beam. But suddenly all I could think about was what I was going to do on floor later in the competition. I shook my head, trying to focus. When I was ready, I took a powerful few steps and launched myself into a round-off, gaining momentum for the dismount. For my dismount, I had to complete a full twist in the air before landing on the mats. I pulled my arms in hard to get the twisting motion. But I could tell I wasn't high enough off the beam. I could see the floor approaching with speed, and I wasn't finished spinning. I hit the ground without completing my turn and stumbled. I staggered forwards and landed on my hands and knees on the mat. Not only would I be penalised for not completing the twist, but I'd also lose points for falling.

I stood up, devastated. My friends gave me sympathetic looks as I shuffled back over to them.

'Don't worry, Abs,' Mae said soothingly. 'There's still vault and floor to go.'

As I choked back tears, I saw the bright neon scoreboard flashing my score to everyone around. There was nowhere to hide. 10.27. It was a bad score. My heart sank as I realised just how much I was going to have to do to keep myself in the running for the top-twelve squad. My vault was a simple vault which I could do well, but there wasn't much going for it in terms of difficulty. To claw my way back into this competition, there was only one solution: nail my floor routine.

# CHAPTER *Ten*

After completing our vault rotation and all doing quite well (with Evie smashing her new vault skill), it was time for floor. Floor was our last apparatus for the day and I needed a big score to make up for my disastrous fall on beam.

All my other friends had nailed their favoured apparatus, even with their added degrees of difficulty. Scarlet had done her floor rotation and performed her new tumbling row with ease. So it was up to me to do the best floor routine of my life – not just to get me into the top twelve, but to keep my promise to my friends.

Coach Ana was standing by the floor. She'd stayed on floor the entire competition, coaching each of the rotations through the apparatus. She quickly glanced over our score card so far, nodding and wincing as she read down the different scores.

'Okay, you're doing well, girls,' she said when she reached the bottom. 'Abby, can I have a quick word?'

My stomach dropped. I sighed and walked over to her as she pulled me away from the other girls.

'I saw your fall on beam,' she said. 'Don't be upset – you've got floor now and it's your best apparatus. You performed this routine beautifully in the last comp I saw you in. But I don't think you should try the double somersault with the twist.'

'But I need the bonus points!' I protested. 'I can't just do a simple routine – even if I do it well I won't get a high enough score.'

'Isn't that better than trying something that you aren't ready to do and ruining the whole routine?'

I looked to the ground. I felt so confused. 'But I promised ...'

'Promised who?' Coach Ana said, frowning.

'My friends. We wanted to do killer routines on our best apparatus and have the highest level of difficulty possible to up our scores.'

Coach Ana sighed and nodded, as if everything had become clear. 'Abby,' she said gently, 'at the end of the day, whose score are they going to hold up on that board when *your* routine is done? Mae's? Anwen's?'

'No, mine,' I said flatly.

'Exactly. You need to take responsibility for your own competition. Remember when you told me what you loved about gymnastics?'

Coach Ana said as she put a hand on my shoulder.

'That I feel free – like I can fly.' I nodded, remembering our chat from the first day in the gym.

'Exactly. Right now you're not flying. You're tying yourself to the ground with a pressure that you don't need. This is *your* comp. Go out there and be the gymnast I know you are. Go out there and love every minute. Feel the music. Soar through the air. Go fly, Abby.'

Tears began to prick my eyes as I nodded. Coach Ana gave me a quick hug and ushered me back over to our group.

'What did she say?' asked Anwen.

'She just told me to do what I need to do,' I said, staring vacantly into the bricks on the wall.

'Abigail Rogers,' the head judge called.

'Right, let's do this,' I said firmly as I stood up to face my routine with Coach Ana's words echoing through my head.

I presented to the judges and walked confidently onto the centre of the blue mats. I stood in my first pose and waited. Suddenly, the music blasted through the speakers – it was *my* music – the music that I loved. I sprung to life, dancing across the mats and launching into the air. I felt like a lead weight had been lifted from my shoulders and legs. I leapt, gracefully and beautifully. I felt fluid and expressive.

I moved to the corner of the mat, ready for my first tumbling row. With a fierceness that I hadn't felt throughout the entire competition, I flipped and soared, landing perfectly on two feet. I could hear the cheers of my friends and the crowd.

My second tumbling row was fast and strong and I also landed it perfectly. Another cheer rose from the crowd. With more leaps and dance moves, I flowed through the rest of my routine like a prima ballerina. Then suddenly, I found myself standing in the corner of the mats, ready for my final tumbling row. This was it. This was where I was meant to do a double full twisting somersault. I glanced briefly at my friends who sat, holding their breath. I caught Coach Ana's eye as she nodded lightly. I waited for the crescendo in the music and ran. I ran with all my might and launched myself into a strong round-off. My flips were strong. *I am free. I can fly.*

Suddenly, my body took over my mind. I launched off the ground and soared through the air. I couldn't control what I was doing – my body had a mind of its own. Instead of tucking into a tight ball for a double somersault, and instead of pulling my arms in to add a twist, I found myself doing something totally different. It was completely unexpected. My body soared through the air in a double layout. It was the ultimate vision of flight – a body stretched out long and straight, suspended in the air for less than half a second like a bird soaring through the sky.

I knew my double layout was high – higher than I've ever tumbled before. The air whipped around my body as I rotated quickly and freely. I landed hard on my feet in a perfect landing. My friends jumped to their feet and the crowd gasped. My music finished and I ended the routine with my final pose.

I presented to the judges and walked off the floor to the hugs of my overjoyed friends.

'What was THAT?' Evie screamed.

Even Scarlet ran over from her beam circuit to give me a hug. 'A double layout? Where did that come from?' she gasped.

I shrugged as Coach Ana came over. 'I don't know! I just – it just felt right.'

Coach Ana shook her head and gave me a quick hug. 'Way to pull out a new skill in the middle of a comp, Abby, are you nuts?!'

I laughed as I turned to my left. There, standing quietly, was Bella. I was ready to ignore her snide remark which was undoubtedly about to come out. 'Abby, can I talk to you?' she asked.

I stepped to the side with Bella as my friends looked on, confused.

'Abby, I just wanted to say thank you. Thank you for saving my beam routine. And ... I'm sorry. I know I've been a complete cow to you ...'

'But why?' I asked angrily. 'I've never done anything to you. But you keep being so mean to me. It's because you think I don't deserve a spot at the Academy, isn't it?'

Bella's eyes widened. 'No! No, that's not it at all, the opposite in fact! It goes back to our audition comp – before we even started at the Academy. I was watching your floor routine with my coach. You were flying across the floor – you looked so beautiful and free. And my coach whispered to me that you were the one to watch. She said you would be my competition here.'

'But I fell in that routine!' I laughed shaking my head.

'It's not about falling or not falling, Abby,' Bella said, shaking her head. 'And then on our first day at the Academy, I heard Coach Ana say exactly the same thing to you – you have the passion and something inside you that can't be taught. And I was jealous. I know I'm a good gymnast, but sometimes I feel like I'm not as natural as you.'

I shook my head, disbelieving. All this time I had been doubting myself. For nothing!

Right at that moment the crowd let out a little gasp and then started cheering. The scoreboard lit up with my floor score: 13.95. It was my highest score and I gasped. It was a huge score, but would it be enough to get me into the top twelve? I was going to have to wait and see.

The podium stood in the middle of the floor with all the girls sitting around it. We jittered nervously as the final results were counted. When they were in Coach Ana read through them, nodding with raised eyebrows. She picked up the cordless microphone and wandered to the centre of the floor.

'Okay, the results are in. First of all, I just want to say a big congratulations to every single one of our gymnasts for competing today.' The parents and siblings in the gallery clapped nervously. 'All of you did an amazing job in your first competition as Academy students.'

I could hear Mae breathing nervously beside me.

'But now, to our place-getters,' Coach Ana said, smiling. 'On bars, in third place, Claudia Cox; second place, Mae Choon; and first place, Annabelle Winton.'

We cheered loudly, especially for Mae. Mae stood proudly as Coach Ana hung the medal around her neck.

‘Beam: third place, Sophie Bell; second place, Isabella Burnetti; first place, Anwen Jones.’

Anwen jumped up and we all whooped as she stood on the podium. She looked tiny on the first place block, but her little smile beamed wider than anyone else’s.

‘Bella has placed already,’ Evie whispered nervously to me.

‘Vault: third place, Evie Brown; second place, Claudia Cox; first place, Scarlet Belyakov.’

Evie gave a whopping ‘Woohoo!’ as she bounded towards the podium. Everyone laughed at her boisterousness.

‘Floor: third place, Isabella Burnetti; second place, Scarlet Belyakov; first place, Abigail Rogers.’

Mae slapped me on the back in congratulations. I stood up, dumbfounded that I’d won floor. I’d even beaten Scarlet. I walked up to the podium and climbed to the top. I could see my mum cheering from the crowd. I scanned around the gallery and saw another smiling face – Evie's brother, Andy, was cheering with his hands above his head. He winked when I caught his eye and my face went bright red.

As Coach Ana approached with my medal, I leant down so she could slip it over my head. It was a small golden medal with the Academy of Sport for Girls emblazoned on the front. It felt cold in my hand and like it was the most precious jewel in the entire world. I smiled broadly as I jumped down from the podium.

'And now, the announcement for our top twelve, Squad A, who will be competing for the school at the State Prelims.' Everyone fell silent and still.

'In no particular order,' Coach Ana said 'congratulations to Claudia Cox, Sophie Bell, Evie Brown, Anwen Jones, Scarlet Belyakov, Isabella Burnetti, Mae Choon, Maisie Cooper, Annabelle Winton, Ava Bently …'

*Two positions left …*

'Amanda Harvey …'

*One position left …*

'and Faith Greenwood …'

My heart sank. My friends immediately stopped high-fiving each other as they realised the truth: they were all in. And I wasn't.

'… who has tied for the twelfth spot with Abigail Rogers,' Coach Ana finished.

*What did she say?*

Mae squealed.

'Abby, you're IN!' yelled Evie. 'The top twelve is a top thirteen!'

I shook my head, confused. I was in! We were all in! My friends jumped into a huddle and fell over into a massive group hug, laughing and cheering.

'Well, we may not have kept Bella out of the top twelve, but we achieved what we wanted – we're ALL in!' giggled Anwen.

I couldn't believe it. I'd made it into the top squad after my first competition. And I was going to train for State Prelims with the best friends anyone could ever ask for.

Evie pulled Anwen and Scarlet over to where Mae and I were standing. We stood in a circle with our arms around each other, laughing with joy.

'Well done, girls!' a voice said from behind us. We broke up our circle to see Coach Ana beaming at us. 'You did it! I'm so proud of you. You've proven to everyone, including yourselves,' she said, raising an eyebrow in my direction, 'that you are true Academy gymnasts.'

I looked around at my four new friends. Anwen, Evie, Scarlet and Mae beamed back at me.

'Gather in, photo time!' sang my mum embarrassingly as she ushered us into a line.

The five of us stood proudly with our arms around each other.

'Say "winners"!' my mum yelled as she pointed the camera at us.

'Winners!' we all sang as our Academy medals jingled around our necks.

# CHARACTER PROFILE

**Name:** Abigail Rogers (but call me Abby!)

**Hair colour:** Brown

**Eye colour:** Blue

**Bestie:** Mae. Mae is the first person I met at the Academy and she's the most loyal person I've ever known. I also love my other training buddies – Evie, the firecracker, Anwen, the sweet little pixie and Scarlet, our sometimes mysterious friend.

**Likes:** Gymnastics, of course! I love floor the best – nothing feels freer than leaping through the air and soaring into a tumbling row. But not a forward tumble. I only like going backwards! I like Art and History at school. I'm actually pretty good at drawing.

**Dislikes:** Forward tumbling (see above!); rips on my hands; stacking on beam; Bella when she's in a bad mood; homework.

**If I couldn't be a famous athlete, I would be . . .** a coach. If I can't do gymnastics, I'll teach it. You can't get me out of the gym that easily!

**If I was at a party, I would be . . .** dancing with my friends.

## ABOUT THE AUTHOR

Ever since she learnt to hold a pen, Laura Sieveking has loved creating stories. She remembers hiding in her room as a six-year-old, writing a series of books about an unlikely friendship between a princess and a bear.

As an adult, Laura has spent the vast majority of her career working in publishing as an editor. After several years, she decided to put down her red pen and open up her laptop to create a series of her own.

The Academy series is a combination of Laura's favourite things – writing, friendship and sport, all of which take her back to her happy childhood memories of gymnastics training and competitions.

Laura lives in Sydney with her husband and two children.

## ACKNOWLEDGEMENTS

A special thank you to Natalie Harvey of Manly Warringah Gymnastics Club for your expert advice in the creation of this book.

And to the gym girls of my youth – thank you for defining and shaping my school days into some of the happiest I've ever had. You are on every page.

## READ ALL THE BOOKS IN
### The Academy of Sport for Girls series.

## SWIMMING

**Can swim queen Delphie keep her winning edge as rivalries and unexpected scandals surface at the Academy?**

Having been at the Academy of Sport for Girls for six months, Delphie Attkinson is living her dream. While attending a state training camp, Delphie and the Year 7 Academy swim squad, come face-to-face with their biggest rival, the National Swim School. Tensions are soon running high in *and* out of the water as the rival schools are forced to train together. But Delphie sees this as an opportunity to learn about the strengths and weaknesses of the Swim School's best swimmers, the unbeatable Ogilvy twins. Surprisingly, Delphie forms a close friendship with one of the sisters, however, in doing so, she uncovers a shocking secret.

Faced with a host of challenges she never thought she would have to encounter, can Delphie make the right choice and retain her all-important swimming crown?

FROM THE AUTHOR OF ELLA AT EDEN
GIRLS SPORTS ACADEMY
Swimming
Delphie's Story
LAURA SIEVEKING

## ATHLETICS

**Can hurdling champion Josie find a way to improve her grades as well as follow her gold medal dreams at the Academy?**

With the Academy of Sport for Girls end-of-year Athletics State Finals fast approaching, golden girl of the track, Josie Ingram, and her teammates are training hard. It seems like nothing can stop them from reaching their dreams. However, when Josie finds out she is falling behind in her schoolwork, her world is turned upside down. If she doesn't improve her grades in the upcoming exams, she won't be allowed to compete at the State Finals! Forced to concentrate on her studies and banned from any track practice sessions, Josie feels like giving up. Everything she has trained for will mean nothing if she can't compete.

Can Josie commit to her schoolwork and hold on to her chances of a podium finish? Or will she accept an easy offer that spells trouble?

FROM THE AUTHOR OF ELLA AT EDEN
GIRLS SPORTS ACADEMY
Athletics
Josie's Story
LAURA SIEVEKING

**Read on for an extract from**
***The Academy of Sport for Girls: Swimming***

# CHAPTER *One*

According to Greek mythology, Delphin was the god of the dolphins. He served the sea-god Poseidon and was sent on special missions for him. He was fast, sleek and beautiful. He was a creature of the water – the sea was his domain. His shining body would glide through the misty depths of the ocean, seeking out whatever Poseidon had sent him to find.

It was a story that ran through my head often. My mum had told it to me over and over as I went to sleep at night. You see, my name is Delphine and, like my namesake Delphin, I too am a creature of the water.

It was obvious from a young age that I was special when it came to the water. I was able to swim by the time I was two years old and by five I was swimming laps with kids twice my age. I was discovered by a coach from a renowned local swim school and he put me in their elite development squad when I was eight. I was training five mornings a week in every season of the year. But it was never a chore. Before the sun had even kissed the horizon, I would be awake in the darkness of my room, packing my swimming bag, ready for training. My poor parents were dragged out of bed at five o'clock in the morning to take me to my squads. But I think it was all worth it for them, as they huddled on the sideline with a rug and a steaming thermos of coffee, to see the glee on my face as I finished another lap. I'd wave to them on the viewing platform, giving them a big thumbs up. They would wave back and smile.

As time went on, juggling school and swimming training became difficult. Training became earlier and earlier in the morning so we could fit in enough sessions alongside school. I loved school, but every afternoon my eyes would be fixated on the classroom clock, willing the little hands to move faster towards home time so I could hit the pool or the beach.

If I wasn't at training, I'd be at the beach with my dad and my three older siblings. My dad is a keen surfer – he once represented Australia in surfing – and all my siblings have been water babies. My two brothers surf competitively and my older sister plays water polo for the state. We live right by the beach and we only feel complete if we have sand between our toes and crunchy sea-salt hair.

I remember my dad driving me to early-morning training one day when I was in Year 5. He said that he and Mum were exhausted by my training schedule as well as looking after the other three kids who had their own gruelling timetables. My heart was in my throat – where was he going with this conversation? In my mind that day, I decided that if he was going to make me quit swimming, I would run away to the ocean and become a mermaid and live in an underwater kingdom for the rest of my days.

Luckily, Dad wasn't asking me to quit swimming at all, which was fortunate as I wasn't exactly sure how to find this underwater kingdom. Instead, he told me about a school in the city that was the best sporting academy for girls in the country – a school where you did your schoolwork but also had time every single day to devote to your chosen sport. Girls from this school went on to the Olympics and other sporting halls of fame. It was called the Academy of Sport for Girls and it sounded like a dream come true.

The Academy was about a forty-minute bus ride from our house. It was also a boarding school, but I wouldn't need to stay there as I lived close enough to just ride the bus each day. This was a huge relief for me, as a life lived far from the beach seemed like no life at all.

Getting into the Academy was tough. I spent the rest of that year training the hardest I'd ever trained in my life. Every other swimming meet seemed irrelevant – the only thing I wanted was to get into this school.

Finally, after swimming meets, interviews and some academic testing, the results were in. They came in the form of a crisp, white envelope with the Academy logo on the top left-hand corner. I remember gazing at the school crest with its four quadrants. I ran my fingers over the images inside the crest – a lion, an eagle, a plume of feathers and the laurel leaves. Underneath were some Latin words which I couldn't read. I clearly remember my dad opening the letter for me – I couldn't look. I scanned his face eagerly, searching for a hint of disappointment or glee.

That was last year.

Which brings me up to this moment.

Here I was, shaking out my arms and legs as I approached the blocks. I glanced down at my Academy swimming costume and smiled. It was navy blue with a white trim and bore the Academy crest on the bottom left hip. I adjusted my swimming cap that had the Academy of Sport for Girls initials on the side. I felt someone squeeze my arm in encouragement. It was Melissa, another member of the 4 x 100-metre relay team. She was the first to swim as our strong backstroke swimmer. She offered me a nervous smile.

Next up would be Bec. Her specialty was breaststroke. She was shy by nature but a force to be reckoned with in the water.

Our butterfly swimmer was Ava. She is the tallest twelve-year-old I've ever seen and one of the best athletes I've met. She could have qualified at the Academy in athletics, basketball or netball, but swimming is her passion.

And then there was me. Delphine. Delphie-Dolphin, as the girls called me. I was the last to race as the fastest 100-metre freestyler at the Academy for our age group.

'Okay, girls, let's do this!' I yelled, jumping up and down. I'd become like the captain of the relay team – Coach Stuart had asked me to be in charge of psyching up the girls before the race. I know exactly why he chose me to do it – I was a ball of energy and positivity and nothing could shake my confidence. I'd always been the loudest person in any room and shyness was not a problem for me. Keeping my mouth shut sometimes was.

Melissa stood on the edge of the pool and took a deep breath. She plopped herself into the water and resurfaced, giving us a big smile. She held on to the side of the pool and adjusted her goggles.

'Time to win, girls, and time to kick some butt!' a voice yelled from the lane next to me. I looked over and saw Annabel Ogilvy clapping loudly to encourage her relay team. Annabel glanced at me with a cold, blank expression, then turned back to her team.

I knew Annabel because she was also the freestyle swimmer for their team. While I was the fastest freestyler at the Academy, she was the fastest freestyler at the National Swim School. They were our biggest rival. In most meets, it was either me or Annabel who took out the 100-metre freestyle gold. We'd swum against them in the qualifiers earlier and Annabel seemed to be swimming a little slower than usual. We qualified first and the National Swim School had come in second. I was quietly hoping maybe they were having an off day.

'Take your mark,' a crackly voice said over the speaker system.

Melissa crouched up against the wall, ready to push off.

*BEEEP!*

The backstroke swimmers launched themselves into the water and the race was in full swing. Melissa's long, lean body undulated through the clear water with her arms stretched out above her head. She'd made a good start.

Suddenly, the erratic splashing began as the backstroke swimmers surfaced. Melissa powered through the water at amazing speed with the Swim School backstroker just half a body behind. Melissa made a good turn and pushed out in front as she swam back towards us in her final lap. As her last arm stroke reached out for the wall, Bec was off.

The frenzied splashing of the backstrokers subsided as the heads of the breaststroke swimmers bobbed up and down in the water. The Swim School breaststroker was probably the best swimmer on their team. She quickly destroyed the lead that Melissa had created in the backstroke leg and overtook Bec at the tumble turn. But Bec wasn't giving up. She kept close to the Swim School swimmer, nipping at her toes the whole lap back.

I wasn't too nervous yet as I knew Ava would be our secret weapon in getting us ahead again on the butterfly leg. As Bec finished, Ava propelled her body into the water and began her thundering butterfly lap. Her wide, strong shoulders pulsed in and out of the water as she drove her body forwards. By the time Ava was heading back up towards our end of the pool, she'd regained the lead. She was a body length ahead of anybody else and I knew all I had to do was finish the job for a win.

I stood on the blocks, energy pumping through my body. It had been a huge day for me – qualifiers and finals in four races and this was my last race of the day. Even though I was exhausted, I knew I could do it.

I glanced to my side and saw Annabel Ogilvy yelling 'C'mon!' as she stood tall, ready to dive. It was going to be between the two of us. Annabel had swum just as much as I had that day, so she should have been equally tired. We were both running on empty tanks, but it was time to pull out any last drops of energy we had left.

As Ava thundered to the end of the pool, I launched myself into a long, graceful dive. The deafening roar of the water in my ears as I hit the pool signalled to my body that it was time to give everything I had. As I began into my freestyle stroke, I knew I had to finish this off for my team. The black line at the bottom of the pool raced by beneath me as I quickly reached the end of my first lap. I could feel Annabel just behind me – an eerie, threatening presence.

As the end of the pool approached, I felt my rhythm was a bit off. My tumble turn was too early and I didn't get maximum push-off for my second lap. I could feel Annabel tumble next to me and shoot out ahead.

I switched it up a gear and began to sprint.

But Annabel was like a rocket. Her swimming seemed far stronger than it had been in the qualifiers.

I knew I had to focus on my own stroke and stop worrying about what was happening in the next lane. I put my head down and channelled every ounce of strength I had left into finishing this race.

As I hurtled towards the finish, I gave it everything. I thumped my hand against the wall, ripped off my goggles and turned to the electronic scoreboard as the winners lit up one by one.

1. The National Swim School
2. The Academy of Sport for Girls
3. College of Sport
4. Hunterville Sports High

I didn't even read the rest of the placings. We hadn't won.

I looked up and saw the Swim School team pull Annabel Ogilvy out of the pool and hug her. They pumped their fists into the air and made a 'number one' sign with their fingers.

My team hoisted me out of the pool and gave me a pat on the back.

'Good swim, Delphie,' Ava said.

'I'm so sorry, guys, I let you down,' I said, shaking my head. I felt terrible.

'Second place is great,' Melissa smiled. 'We'll get them next time.'

As we moved to the side and grabbed our towels, I saw Annabel pull off her swim cap. Her long, dark hair tumbled down from her ponytail as she rubbed her face with her towel.

'You did it!' squealed a voice behind us.

Another girl, of identical height to Annabel – and with the same long, dark hair – ran up and hugged her. It was her identical twin sister, Ashley. Ashley was also one of the Swim School's better swimmers, although she wasn't quite as unbeatable as her sister, which was why she didn't swim in the relay. The Ogilvy sisters stood side by side, holding hands. They were towering girls, standing together in a seemingly unbreakable wall. One thing was for sure, if the Academy was going to take down the Swim School any time soon, we had to start beating the twins. Especially Annabel.